CW00969619

Praise for *The B*

"Great ideas don't just happen. Good leaders create a purposeful environment where brilliant ideas are generated, captured, and implemented. *The Bright Idea Box* is part inspiration, part workbook, part resource, and a book everyone can learn from."

— Daniel H. Pink,
Author of *TO SELL IS HUMAN* and *DRIVE*

"This powerful, practical book shows you how to motivate, inspire, and get the very best out of each person in your company."

— Brian Tracy, Author of *Full Engagement*

"More and more organizational leaders are realizing that the most efficient and effective way to stimulate growth is to engage the existing workforce and cultivate innovation from within. Jag Randhawa's *The Bright Idea Box* teaches you how to create practical, viable programs that will transform the company and the bottom line!"

— Marshall Goldsmith, America's Preeminent Executive
Coach (*Fast Company* magazine)

"It is almost a no-brainer to read this book to MASTER six steps for creating a bottom-up innovation program that not only retains your best employees but engages them to provide meaningful contributions to business growth. Not-put-downable from cover-to-cover, forcing you to reach for your yellow highlighter at every page."

— Anurag Agrawal, CEO, Techaisle

"If you are looking to reinvigorate your workforce to achieve your organizational goals, this book is the most important resource to help you get maximum results!"

— **Patrick Snow, International Best Selling Author of** ***Creating Your Own Destiny*** **and** ***The Affluent Entrepreneur***

"Jag Randhawa's book is the rare gem that not only outlines a new concept but also manages to make the process tangible and easy to adopt. Jag makes a compelling case for his Six-Step Master Innovation Program. He has test-driven his process and speaks from experience. He backs up the reasoning for each step with case studies and research and concludes each chapter with a very helpful guide to get started. An essential guide to Innovation Management. Highly recommended."

— **Frauke Schorr, Ph.D.,**
Founder and Principal at Centered Leadership Institute

"Jag is one of those exceptional technologists, who demonstrate an exceptional understanding of people and how to motivate them to collaborate and excel. In this book, combining a timely synopsis of current management thought leadership and his own refinement and implementation of best practices, Jag provides a handbook for empowering employees, which leads to an explosion of engagement and innovation. This step-by-step guide is a valuable addition to any leader's library, providing insights into a possible, practical, and rewarding innovation process. A great return on your investment of time."

— **Sophia Abramovitz, Program Management Executive,**
CEO Norton Enterprises International, Inc.

"*The Bright Idea Box* provides readers with a simple secret "how-to" formula for employee engagement, plus dozens of invaluable tips, tricks, and techniques learned from many of the innovative giants in the marketplace, who put employee engagement and empowerment at the heart of their business models."

— **Susan Friedmann, CSP, International Bestselling Author of** ***Riches in Niches: How to Make it BIG in a small Market***

"*The Bright Idea Box* is a must read for any business that wants to take productivity to the next level. Jag lays out a step-by-step process for increasing employee engagement and creating a culture of innovation. Highly recommended!"

— **Dr. Levi Murray, Entrepreneur and Author of**
Succeeding by Choice

"Employees are the most important, yet often most underutilized resource for continuous innovation. Jag's book *The Bright Idea Box* shows how companies can engage employees in developing new ideas that not only engage them but also improve the business."

— **Michelle Graham, CEO and Co-Founder,**
Graham & Graham LLC

"Jag Randhawa has created a program that will take your business to new levels—accessing the brilliant ideas of employees to help leaders create innovation that keeps their organizations not just thriving but leading on the cutting edge. Jag has done the research and pulled it all together in an easy-to-access book. Jag helps you access the brilliance that is sitting right there in your company."

— **Donna Price, Business Strategist, Author of** *Employee*
Coaching for Business Success & Launching Your Dreams

"This book is a must read for any employer, leader, or manager who wants to engage his or her employees in innovative practices."

— **H.C. Joe Raymond, Life Coach, Speaker, and Author of**
Embracing Change from the Inside Out

"One of the great challenges for any business is retaining its most valuable assets, its employees. In *The Bright Idea Box*, Jag Randhawa shares priceless information to keep your employees engaged in their work. Being a 'stakeholder' and feeling like an integral part of the company is one of the four pillars of Conscious Capitalism. The future success of business depends on the principles in this book. Pick it up today and follow the exercises in each chapter."

— **Mark Porteous, Author of**
Maximizing the Human Experience

YOUR LEADERSHIP BLUEPRINT FOR BUSINESS SUCCESS

The Bright
IDEA BOX

A Proven System to Drive
Employee Engagement and Innovation

AVIVA
PUBLISHING

Jag Randhawa

Hardcover ISBN: 978-1-938686-81-8
Paperback ISBN: 978-1-940984-06-3
eBook ISBN: 978-1-940984-07-0
1. Leadership. 2. Organizational Change. 3. Employee Motivation. I. Title.
Library of Congress # 2013955113

Editor: Tyler Tichelaar
Cover & Interior Book Design: Fusion Creative Works

Every attempt has been made to source properly all quotes.
Published by Aviva Publishing, New York
First Edition

For additional copies visit:
www.TheBrightIdeaBox.com

CONTENTS

To my lovely daughters—Jasmine and Leah

Foreword

PATRICK SNOW

When I began my career right out of college in corporate America, I quickly learned that some jobs were better than others, and it all seemed to come back to the level of participation, respect, and caring given by the senior managers and or company owners.

I also often wondered why some of my coworkers flourished in their jobs and felt alive, while others constantly complained and jumped from one job to another without ever being able to build successfully any kind of significant career.

What I learned is that there are two major reasons for worker apathy. Either the manager or owner does not care about the workers, or the employee has a bad attitude, or perhaps both.

What I learned over the years is that the single greatest asset a company possesses is not its intellectual property, its products, or its services. But rather, it is its people! The employees who make up an organization have always been and will always be the most important assets a company possesses. Those organizations that know this to be true all succeed, and those that don't ultimately perish. I eventually quit my last job at age thirty-five and have successfully built my own company since then. In doing so, I have always remembered that my team is the greatest asset to my organization!

When employees are not treated well, or given the opportunity for advancement, the problem isn't that many of these workers quit their jobs and *leave*. Rather, they quit their jobs and *stay*! They stay on the payroll long after quitting. Then, not only do they do a poor job at work, and at serving the organization's needs and the clients' needs, but they even quit on themselves. Therefore, the major question becomes: How can an employer inspire his or her team to greatness while continuing to serve the customer? This question has plagued companies for years.

In this powerful book by Jag Randhawa, you will learn the answer to this question and much, much more. You will learn why employees either quit and *leave*, or quit and *stay*! You will learn that engaged employees are more productive, build better relationships with customers, eliminate corporate politics, and develop more ideas that advance the organization to its ultimate goals, visions, and objectives.

In *The Bright Idea Box*, Jag introduces a *Master Innovation Program* that companies can use to engage employees to grow the business better. You will learn how to create a platform that encourages employees to come up with brilliant ideas to grow the business, create operational efficiencies, reduce costs, and improve customer service.

Furthermore, this book shows how companies can create a competitive edge using their existing products and resources without having to invent new ones. This book teaches you how to engage employees in an idea-generation process that adds value to the company, customers, and shareholders.

Throughout this book, you will learn that employees are most engaged when they feel their input is valued and they have an opportunity to make a difference. When you create such a framework for observation and input, it makes your employees feel part of something bigger than themselves, and it motivates them to do even more!

Jag Randhawa is one of the most brilliant business thinkers on our planet today. Not only is he an amazing thinker, but he also has an innate passion for improving things. As a result, he is an *even* better doer! He is a husband, the father of two daughters, and genuinely one of the kindest men I know.

When you follow the principles laid out in this book, your organization will soar to new heights. So get out a pen and paper, jot down lots of notes, and allow Jag's six-step *Master Innovation Program* to take your organization to the next level. Not only will you experience a great chemistry and a bond with your employees or coworkers, but your customers will all experience the difference as a result.

So put on your seat belt and get ready for an amazing ride. You are about to embark on a journey that will do amazing things not only for your leadership skills, but also your career. You can become that force of change within your organization that gets you noticed by the senior executives. Your life is about to change for the better, and I am confident that you will benefit and be pleased with the results! Enjoy....

Patrick Snow

International Best-Selling Author of *Creating Your Own Destiny* and *The Affluent Entrepreneur*

Introduction

Connecting The Dots

Great vision without great people is irrelevant.
— Jim Collins

In 1979, a pioneering company developed a concept that changed the computer industry forever, and the way we live and do things—a graphical user interface called "Windows" and a little device that can perform computer commands on those windows called the "mouse." Xerox PARC, an innovation arm of Xerox Corporation, invented the most pivotal concept in computer history, but it failed to capitalize on the potential of its invention. As a matter of fact, nobody on the streets will even remotely associate Xerox with computers, let alone pioneering the computer industry. Instead, it was Apple Computers that led the computer industry's revolution by borrowing the idea from Xerox.

It is never an idea, technology, market forces, or access to capital that makes a company innovative. What differentiates an innovative company from an average company is the people working inside the company. Their drive, engagement, and close alignment to a common vision are perhaps the greatest predictors of success and continuous innovation. The company's success appears to be founded on a grand idea, but often it is a collection of ideas developed over time. Innovative companies engage in a relentless pursuit of ideas, big or small, to improve their products and create a culture where every employee is engaged in the idea hunt.

Researchers have long argued that a strong correlation exists between employee engagement and innovation. A highly engaged workforce can transform an average company to an innovative company, while a disengaged workforce can kill a great company. I don't think anyone disputes this finding, but there is a strong disconnect between this understanding and common business practices. In a recent global survey conducted by IBM, CEOs ranked innovation as their top priority and focus for the future. Innovation is on everyone's mind. According to *The Wall Street Journal*, in 2012, companies used the word "innovation" more than 33,528 times in their annual and quarterly reports. How many times do you think they used the term "employee engagement"? Innovation is the hottest buzzword in the business world, but employee engagement is almost an afterthought. Is it any wonder that Gallup Polls indicate that only 26 percent of employees are actively engaged?

Before we dive any deeper into employee engagement and innovation, I want to invite you to ponder a few questions: How engaged are the employees at my company? What is my company's employee retention rate? When was the last time an employee did something out of the ordinary to effect the top line or bottom line? Do employees walk with their heads up and greet people with a smile or an "I am too busy" look? How do they handle customer complaints? Do they take ownership and try to solve problems, or do they push them down to another department or employee? Does my company share a sense of camaraderie, or is it more of a political silo? Do employees prefer to follow procedures and be told what to do, or are they always ready to do whatever it takes to make the company more successful? Do employees understand the relationship between the company's success and their own success?

If answering any of these questions makes your heart sink, don't worry; you are not alone. I have battled with many of these issues, and if the Gallup Polls carry any weight, the whole world is struggling with these issues.

I live in Silicon Valley, and I have seen the birth and demise of many tech giants. The 2001 dot-com bust nearly wiped out all Internet companies, but one company defied all the odds—Google. Google did not just survive the dot-com collapse, but it has thrived through all the recessions since. Google seems to have a war chest of ideas, and it launches more products than I can even remember. What is even more interesting is that some of the best products Google has launched since its famous search engine service were all employee ideas. Google's culture seems to attract some of the best and brightest employees who are driven and work hard to make the company successful. All these facts are very intriguing, but like many others, I ignored the whole Google buzz for years, attributing its success mostly to a single good idea, market timing, tech culture, and pure luck. Even though I ran an Information Technology department, I saw no resemblance between Google and an insurance company, and I never bothered to study its culture. Besides,

Google seems to have all the money in the world, so it can afford to give its employees such a long leash to experiment and work on their hobby projects. Most of us don't have that luxury. Until recently, I would have never thought that a non-tech company could create a Google-like culture where employees come up with ideas to grow the company.

This view changed completely when I learned about a Brazilian company named Brasilata where employees submit ideas to improve their products and processes. Brasilata has won many industry awards, has been ranked among the top twenty innovators, and was rated the best place to work in Brazil. Brasilata is a steel can manufacturing company that competes in a very mature and commoditized business. How can a steel can manufacturing company instill a Google-like culture? For me, Brasilata was both a hope and a challenge at the same time. If a steel can manufacturing company can do it, I had no excuse to procrastinate and ignore the Silicon Valley culture all around me. As I embarked on this discovery, I uncovered that some of the most innovative companies like Apple, Google, Amazon, Starbucks, P&G, W.L. Gore, 3M, Zappos, Whole Foods, and many more, use a very similar framework to out-innovate their competition. These companies put employee engagement and empowerment at the heart of their business models and have led their respective industries by leaps and bounds. The secret formula for employee engagement, as it turned out, is rather simple—encourage employees to come up with ideas that will add value to customers or the company. This process creates a win-win situation that makes employees feel like an integral part of the company, while improving the business results. Innovative companies view their employees as the eyes on the field, and they use their knowledge and insights to develop more attractive and profitable products.

This book offers a framework to create such a program, in which employees submit ideas to create operational efficiencies, improve business processes, increase customer satisfaction, and grow the business. This book mirrors the program I created at my work and the companies I helped in creating this program. The book outlines very simple step-by-step instructions that anyone can use to spur bottom-up innovation regardless of the size and nature of business. Throughout the book, I share personal examples as well as stories of different companies from a diverse set of industries, but there is plenty of room for you to bring your own ideas to the table and tailor the program to meet your unique business needs. My goal is to outline a very simple recipe that you can follow to jumpstart your innovation efforts.

This book is intended for the business leader who wants to make innovation everyone's job. I have tried my best to create a "how-to" book that will walk you through the steps of creating an innovation program that fosters creativity and encourages employees to go above and beyond the call of duty to make the company successful. Creating such a program will initiate a cultural shift that empowers and engages employees to grow their careers and the business. It creates a culture of innovation, in which every individual in the organization is constantly thinking of ways to add value for customers and the company. This book is equally resourceful for entrepreneurs who know that building the right culture from day one will fuel long-term success.

Some of you might be wondering "Why this book?" and "Why you, Jag?" My innovation journey started after the 2008 financial meltdown, but it wasn't exactly a straight path. Just like many others, after the 2008 recession, I had to cut costs and lay-off employees, which forced me to figure out how to do more with less. Additionally, I managed technology staff in the heart of Silicon Valley, and I was afraid I would lose some of my best employees. The technology sector was still doing well, and I was concerned my staff would leave for better opportunities. I wanted to retain my remaining team members, and I was desperately looking for ways to keep them engaged. This need pushed me to learn new ways to engage employees. During this time, I read many books on employee engagement and leadership in the hope of learning some tips and tricks to keep my team engaged, motivated, and focused. I diligently practiced many of the techniques I learned. One of these techniques was to invite employees to suggest ideas that could help me cut costs, improve service standards, and add value to the business. This technique worked like magic. My team not only came up with many good ideas, but it also worked hard to implement them. Some of these ideas made significant contributions to the company's operations, customer experience, and bottom-line profit. Not only did I retain my staff, but in 2012, my team reported 92 percent employee engagement in a survey conducted by an outside company. This taught me the greatest lesson of my life and gave me the confidence and courage to launch a company-wide bottom-up innovation program.

This book is heavily influenced by my personal experiences and the efforts I put into creating this program, but just as Apple did not invent the Personal Computer with graphical user interface, I did not invent the principles discussed in this book. Apple took the concepts from Xerox, and it bridged the gaps between the various loose ends of technology and user experience to create a Personal Computer that was easy to use and highly functional. Similarly, I have tried to create a very simple and easy to implement framework for innovation that bridges the gap between innovation and employee engagement.

At the point of this writing, there is no book on the market, to my knowledge, that walks you through the process of creating an employee-powered innovation program. I frequently speak on this topic, and people always ask me where they can find more information about this program. Which one book would I recommend? The emphasis is always on "one-book." Most of these people are busy business leaders who don't necessarily have years to spare reading and doing research. They know "why" they need to foster a culture of innovation, but they can use some guidance on "how" to get started. Above all, why reinvent the wheel? This book is not meant to persuade anyone why he or she needs innovation, but rather to show how to get started on this journey. With global competition and dispersed resources, business executives are busier than ever. I have intentionally kept this book small to respect my reader's time.

It took me four years of reading books on innovation, leadership, and employee engagement, and subsequently experimenting with different methodologies and tactics, to develop this program. I am confident that if you spend that much time reading and experimenting, you'll come up with a plan that will fit in perfectly with your company needs. But if you don't have years to wait, then pick up this book and follow the recipe. The innovation program outlined in this book is based on a real program, with real business outcomes. The program has been tested and refined over the years to address real business challenges. That said, I have tried my best not to toot my own horn and make this book about me. I have cited examples of my work only to reinforce key points, give real life examples, and avoid becoming too theoretical.

This book is divided into three sections.

Part One—The Innovation

Part Two—The Program

Part Three—The Engagement

Even though the book's primary objective is to walk you through the steps of creating a bottom-up innovation program, I feel it is necessary for you and me to have a common understanding of innovation. In the first section, we will take a deeper dive into understanding what innovation is and how innovation is much more than just developing new products. We will explore the different types of innovation, the sources of innovation, how innovation applies to the service industry, and finally, connect the dots between employee engagement and innovation.

Part Two of the book is all about creating the program. This section is more practical and pragmatic than the first and third sections of the book. In this section, I will walk you through the six steps of the M.A.S.T.E.R. innovation program.

Mobilize: Step 1—Creating the mission and objectives of the program, and identifying the most appropriate domains of innovation for your business.

Amass: Step 2—Developing easily accessible means for collecting ideas.

Support: Step 3—Supporting and encouraging employees through various means.

Triage: Step 4—Creating a committee that will be responsible for screening and prioritizing ideas.

Execute: Step 5—Developing an overarching approach to implement ideas.

Recognize: Step 6—Recognizing employees for their ideas, efforts, and contributions.

Part Three of the book addresses the employee engagement and cultural aspect of the program. This program relies on the voluntary involvement of employees, and such a program cannot be successful without someone championing the program. So I will share some ideas on how to lead such an initiative and get employees excited so they will participate in the program. We will discuss the role of leadership, employee development, tools for innovative thinking, and the importance of bringing all layers of management onboard to succeed in this type of cultural shift. I will share some practical tips and techniques for rolling out the program to all employees and enticing them to submit ideas.

In the appendices, I have listed examples of some companies that use different programs to engage employees and develop innovative products. I have listed these companies to give you more examples and ideas, so you can tailor the program to best meet your business' unique organizational and cultural needs. A lot of literature is available on all of these companies, so it shouldn't be a problem to dive deeper to learn their particular techniques. I have also listed some of my favorite books related to the topic of innovation and explained why I recommend them. These books are absolute gems and I highly recommend reading all of them.

By the end of this book, you should have a good framework that you can use either as is or with slight tweaks to better meet your business needs. At the end of every chapter, I have included some questions for you to answer. Do your best to answer them as you read. At the end of the book, I will show you how you can use your answers to develop a program that will fit your unique business needs.

Let's get started!

Innovation simply isn't as unpredictable as many people think.
There isn't a cookbook yet, but we're getting there.

— Clayton Christensen

- Part One -

THE INNOVATION

Chapter 1

Leveraging What You Got

Do what you can, with what you have, where you are.
— Theodore Roosevelt

Imagine you are the leader of an established automaker that has done well in the past, but the recent economic turmoil has brought everything to a halt. You cannot sustain current salaries, inventories, and operational costs. You are forced to lay off employees, cut salaries, and close plants. Your challenge is to figure out how to revive the company. No, I am not asking you "how to save Detroit." This story is not new; nor is it unique to the auto industry. Businesses face these challenges all the time. I know because I have been through this cycle twice in the last ten years. And maybe this is your struggle too.

Little over a half-century ago, a small Japanese automaker was struggling with many of these challenges. World War II devastated Japan's infrastructure, economy, and people. Rampant inflation made the Yen worthless, and collecting on debts was nearly impossible. Toyota, then a new hatchling of a company, barely ten years old, faced challenges that many of us face today. At that time, Toyota's rivals in the United States, mainly Ford and GM, had no cash problems and were enjoying a large U.S. and international market. Toyota's market was very small, and it couldn't afford to build multiple plants to take advantage of automation and batch efficiencies. To compete with international giants like Ford and GM and survive in the turbulent economy, Toyota developed a unique approach to manufacturing called the Toyota Production System (TPS). The primary goal of the TPS was to minimize waste in production, reduce defects, and create efficiencies. Unlike its western rivals, which relied on experts to improve quality and efficiency, Toyota enrolled its employees in the relentless pursuit of quality and efficiency. "Toyota believed its first-line employees could be more than cogs in a soulless manufacturing machine. If given the right tools and training, they could be problem solvers, innovators and change agents. Toyota saw the necessary genius to drive operational excellence, quality, and innovation in its workforce," said Gary Hamel, American management expert.

Rather than engineering the system to the finest details to meet challenges, Toyota asked its employees to help identify waste and bottlenecks in its production system. Toyota systematically empowered all employees to find, fix, or escalate problems in the production plant. Even the lowly guy down at the assembly line can pull the cord to stop production if he spotted a problem. Every little, incremental improvement suggested by front-line employees added up to massive improvement in the overall quality of Toyota's cars. In addition, employee involvement and respect for employee input created a unique culture of cooperation, consultation, work ethic, ownership, and engagement at Toyota. This unique partnership with employees transformed Toyota from a struggling small-town company into an icon of quality—and the most profitable automaker in the world.

Toyota is not the only company to profit from a high level of employee engagement. According to Gallup, companies in the top decile of employee engagement outperform their peers by 147 percent in earnings per share and have a 90 percent better growth trend than their competition. Engaged employees are more productive, profitable, and safer; create stronger customer relationships; and stay longer with their companies. Gallup research indicates that employee engagement is the most powerful factor in promoting "out-of-the-box" ideas to improve business processes, customer relationships, and bottom-line profits. Come to think of it, this all sounds like common sense, and I don't think anyone will dispute Gallup's findings.

This begs a very important question: How are we doing on employee engagement?

Gallup conducts employee engagement surveys on a regular basis, but unfortunately, the results are rather grim. Employee engagement is on a continuous decline. Gallup's 2012 employee engagement survey reported that in the United States, less than 26 percent of employees are actively engaged, 57 percent are not engaged, and 18 percent are actively disengaged. In today's fiercely competitive world, where businesses are looking for a few points of profit, having 74 percent of employees disengaged is like having a sinkhole in your backyard. This is not an isolated phenomenon to the United States, but rather a global problem. Gallup's 2011 *State of the Global Workplace* report, which surveyed more than 47,000 employees in 120 countries, indicated that only 11 percent are engaged, 62 percent are disengaged, and 27 percent are actively disengaged. If you are interested in stats for your country, please go to www.Gallup.com and search for employee engagement by country.

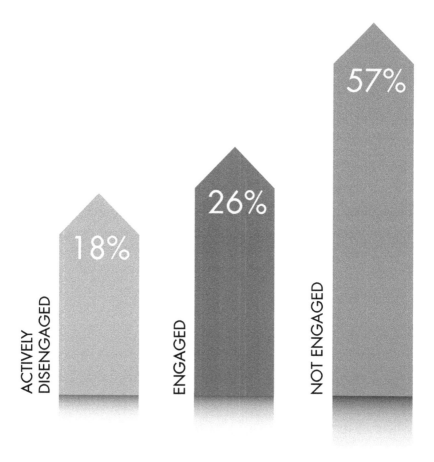

Gallup 2012 U.S. Employee Engagement Results

Forrester analysts Josh Bernoff and Ted Schadler reached a very similar conclusion in their research. They published their results in their book *Empowered*, which suggests that, on average, an organization has about 20 percent HERO Employees (engaged), 34 percent Locked-Down Employees, another 34 percent Disenfranchised employees, and 13 percent Rogue employees (actively disengaged).

If you create a profile of all of your employees, I am confident your own intuitive judgment will reach a similar conclusion. The numbers may not match, but you will find a group of employees who are actively engaged and constantly thinking of ways to advance the company. You will also find a group of disengaged employees who always get in the way of others who want to do better work. These disengaged employees want to do the minimum and resist any change that will expose their secrets or push them out of their comfort zones. Then there is a large group of employees who come to work to collect their paychecks and do what they are told. If there are no incentives, they will find no reason to do their best or go out of their way to do something to help customers or colleagues. These employees will use their job descriptions as excuses to justify their actions and avoid doing any extra work beyond their job requirements. I am sure you have heard some variation of "You need to call the finance department to check on your payment status. Let me transfer you to Sally in Finance." These dynamics become even more prevalent as companies start to grow in size and employees feel disconnected from management and the company's mission.

Employee engagement statistics paint a very grim picture of the current state of business, but they also present an opportunity for excellence. Highly innovative companies have figured out this secret. They put human capital at the center of their business. These companies hire and train employees to think and act like problem solvers and innovators. Jeff Bezos, the founder and CEO of Amazon, is famous for asking interviewees to give examples of innovative work they have done in their lives. It does not have to be job related. It could be anything, such as discovering a new way to load the dishwasher for efficiency, modifying a car for performance, or writing a software encryption algorithm for enhanced security. Google, McKinsey, P&G, and Apple have developed their own variations of problem solving aptitude tests to help them hire the right employees. Every company on earth faces similar challenges; every project or new initiative runs into similar problems. The outcome of these challenges can be a complete failure or an innovative alternative, depending on how the people working inside the company respond to everyday challenges. Disengaged employees will give up and look for someone to blame, while engaged employees will look for alternatives to move the project forward. Companies like Google pay extra attention to their human capital. Ingenious ideas can create a competitive advantage at a point in time, but long-term success depends on evolutionary advantage over time. The right organizational culture enables these evolutionary advantages and fuels long-term success.

Now, let's face the reality—most companies are not like Amazon, Apple, or Google. Most leaders inherit their workforce, and the dysfunctional culture that comes with it. Forget about innovation; many leaders struggle with engaging employees to do their jobs properly and on time. Office politics and functional silos add to these impediments. Almost all leaders are expected to perform miracles with existing resources and limited capital. None have the luxury to replace the entire workforce with more innovative employees. They have to make do with what they have been given.

The good news is that you don't radically need to overhaul your company to start your transformation journey. As a matter of fact, it is not even recommended. This book will offer techniques to elevate the level of your current workforce so you can do more with what you have. It will show you how to find some small patches of fertile ground in your current workforce and use them to sow the seeds of innovation. In your workforce, you already have employees who are highly engaged, passionate about the company, and driven by opportunity. To get started, you need to focus on these engaged employees and create means to harness their energy and desire to make a difference. Once you have some successes, you can turn your attention to those sitting on the borderline by showcasing the work of engaged employees. Success is contagious. Everyone wants to look good and show the world their unique talents. Creating opportunities to showcase their talents will draw people to go above and beyond the call of duty. Slowly and surely, the creative juices will start flowing through the entire organization. Once you have good momentum in the program, peer pressure will force disengaged employees to perform or leave. In time, you will have a company of innovators.

Very few companies create means whereby the employees carrying out tasks can provide input on how to improve them. Management often assumes that employees will raise the issue if they see a problem, but it seldom happens that way. As companies grow in size, the communication gap between the strategic intent and execution grow disproportionately. The intent behind the processes and projects gets lost in the translation. I have heard so many employees saying, "But this is our company policy," with little consideration as to why the policy was created and how their actions counter the reason why the policy was initiated.

Another big roadblock is the mid-managers whose job it is to make sure that employees follow the company's procedures correctly. Managers internalize processes and go to extremes to enforce policies and procedures. Employees become afraid that they might offend the boss by pointing out a problem in the process or trying something that deviates from policy. Line level supervisors and managers get so caught up in the enforcement of processes that they rarely take the time to explain the rationale behind the process. At other times, when employees do raise a concern or an idea to improve the processes, they get shot down in the name of efficiency or for the hassle of making the change. More often, employees are discouraged from pointing out problems since it may make their supervisors look bad. All the management practices work against employees pointing out problems, and sometimes they outright discourage employee involvement in business improvements.

The Bright Idea Box is about creating a program that makes it easier for employees to suggest new ideas, and that encourages employees to develop ideas that can improve the business and add value for customers. The framework and techniques shared in this book can help you overcome many of the challenges and objections. I will share how to leverage tools and processes to create transparency, accountability, and trust, which are essential elements in making the program successful. I will show you how to build recognition into the program to keep the momentum going, and how to position the program so it is not seen as a threat by managers and naysayers.

Creating such a program has an amazing effect on employee engagement. Let's assume for a moment that you get absolutely no good ideas out of this program; then, you will still benefit from increased employee engagement. Establishing this program creates a new sense of worth among the employees, which, by itself, will increase their engagement. They will feel that you value their input—that they are intellectual human beings and their work makes a difference to their company's bottom line. They will feel they are an integral part of the organization and not a dumb or easily replaceable component. Employee engagement increases trust between management and employees. Every job is important in an organization, and every job can be done better. You need to communicate that to employees. Ask them to look for ways to improve functions, processes, and products. If you feel there is any particular role that is not important or could not be improved, you are not thinking hard enough. Sometimes the problem lies in the definition of the role, and at other times, it is the person in that role. Take appropriate actions to make sure you address the actual problem.

Employee disengagement is a growing problem in the twenty-first century. The Bright Idea Box innovation program can help reverse that trend. The program rewards engaged employees who are doing great work by showcasing their work and bringing their ideas forward. Public recognition calls to the inner desire to be appreciated and recognized by peers. Humans have an innate desire to look good. This program makes employees look good. They become the business heroes. The desire to show off creates a healthy competition for ideas. In addition, people work harder when they are working on their own ideas. They want their project to succeed.

Suddenly, they are working for pride and not for a paycheck. When their projects make a difference to the company's growth, employees feel good about being part of something larger than themselves. All of this propels the company forward. It creates a self-sustaining cycle that adds momentum to the company.

Every idea, big or small, incremental or radical, will bring you a step closer to becoming innovative. People think that innovation is about creating the next breakthrough product, but they miss out on huge opportunities to differentiate through continuous improvement in their current product offerings. If you are feeling that this does not sound like innovation, it is. In the next chapter, we will dive deeper into understanding what innovation is and explore different ways your company can be innovative.

RECAP

- The key factor that distinguishes innovative companies is employee engagement.

- Employee engagement is at an all-time low.

- Employees are the most important asset of any organization.

- Engage employees on a higher level by asking them to generate ideas that add value to the company, customers, and stakeholders.

- Bottom-up innovation is an excellent employee engagement tool.

- Ask employees for help and develop the means for employees to contribute beyond their job responsibilities.

Chapter One Exercises

Create a profile of employee engagement at your company.

Q1. Actively Engaged Employees—What percentage of employees regularly go above and beyond to make the company successful?

_____

_____

Q2. Passively Engaged Employees—What percentage of employees are captives of paychecks, who would leave in a heartbeat for a small increase in compensation?

_____

_____

_____

Q3. Disengaged Employees—What percentage of employees hide behind procedures and job descriptions, always have something negative to say, and often get in the way of others trying to do a better job?

_____

_____

_____

_____

Q4. What programs does your company currently use to engage employees?

_____

_____

_____

Q5. Do your employees suggest ideas to improve business functions? If an employee has an idea, how will he or she voice that idea? Does that process encourage employees to submit ideas?

_____

_____

_____

Chapter 2

Debunking the Innovation Myth

Creativity is about thinking new things.
Innovation is about doing new things.
— Theodore Levitt

In business, innovation is the mingling of new and existing ideas to add value for customers, the company, and the marketplace. The results of innovation can emerge as a new or improved product, a new management strategy, lowered cost, added convenience for customers, or selling existing products in new ways or to new markets. This definition, unfortunately, completely kills the romance of innovation. When we think of innovation, we imagine a lone genius holding a lightbulb in his hand, which conjures up notions like an "aha moment." For most, innovation is the byproduct of breakthrough inventions. This raises a very important question:

Do you have to invent something to be innovative?

Most people reflexively think "Yes." People associate innovation with invention. This strong association and the belief that one must invent something to be innovative paralyze many individuals and companies, who, consequently, never set foot on the road to becoming innovative.

While the two words, innovation and invention, are related, you don't have to invent something to be innovative. Some of the most successful and highly innovative companies, including Apple, Starbucks, Toyota, Amazon, Google, and eBay, were not the first to develop the core products. Take Toyota, for example. Toyota is recognized as being among the most innovative companies in the world, but Toyota did not invent the car; the company built a few basic models and then relentlessly improved its cars through continuous improvements. Similarly, Netflix did not invent the DVD rental business, yet the company changed the way we rent and watch movies. Starbucks did not invent the coffee shop, yet the company revived the declining coffee industry. All of these companies changed their respective industries without inventing the core product.

People are often looking for that "aha moment," the "genius idea," or that "game-changing product" that will captivate the market. Just as people obsess over winning the lottery, business leaders obsess over finding breakthrough ideas. In the process, many ignore the importance of adding value to existing products and services. Sure, breakthrough ideas can put you on the map, but there is no guarantee that it will keep you there. The essence of innovation is to add value for customers. Inventions that wow people, but don't add value, rarely survive for long, and they often end up costing more money than they add to the bottom line. For an invention to become innovation, it must add value for customers. The value can come through lowered cost, new features, aesthetics, convenience, ease of use, enhanced experience, or meeting emotional needs. Sometimes the value comes in the form of helping customers make more money, attain goals, or safeguard valuables.

During my presentations, I often ask the audience to name a few innovative companies. Apple, almost always, wins the popularity contest. I agree. Apple is a very innovative company. As a matter of fact, I witnessed the resurrection of Apple after Steve Jobs returned to head the company he had founded. If you lived in Silicon Valley and worked in the high-tech industry in the '90s, Apple's rebound was pretty hard to miss. Shortly after Jobs returned, Apple reclaimed its innovative title and once again changed the computing industry for good. But what did Apple invent? The iPod, iPhone, iPad? Yes, Apple invented these brand names. But, did it invent the MP3 player, the touch-screen phone with Internet connection, or the tablet?

Invention does not equal Innovation

The iPod was Apple's signature product. It helped turn the company around—from near bankruptcy to one of the most valued companies in the world. When Apple introduced the iPod in November of 2001, it was not the first portable MP3 player. As a matter of fact, the market was flooded with MP3 players. Prior to the iPod, most of the popular MP3 players used solid state memory to store songs, which, at that time, did not have much storage capacity. These flash drives were sold in sizes of only a few hundred megabytes, so MP3 players could not hold more than a few CDs. Apple, on the other hand, launched the iPod with a micro hard drive with a 5GB capacity, which, at that time, was a truly a "wow" and "genius" idea. Apple marketed the iPod with the slogan "1,000 songs in your pocket," and many, including myself, credited Apple for creating this amazing device that could hold so many songs. Putting a micro hard drive in an MP3 player was a very smart idea.

However, a lawsuit filed by Creative Labs revealed that Apple did not invent the idea of using micro hard drives in MP3 players. Creative Labs, a Singapore based consumer electronics company, was the first company to come up with the idea of using a micro hard drive and many of the other features used in the iPod. This fact became public knowledge only when Apple settled a lawsuit with Creative Labs for $100 million. This was shocking news to Apple loyalists and admirers who had credited Apple with inventing the high capacity MP3 player.

So, while Apple is not necessarily a company at the forefront of invention, without question, it is a very innovative company. Many industry experts and scholars have ranked Apple among the most innovative companies in history. So what makes Apple innovative?

The answer lies in the execution of the iPod idea. Apple neither invented the MP3 player nor the concept of using a micro hard drive. What Apple did was marry the disparate pieces of technology in a way that created compelling value for consumers. Apple took an existing idea with market potential and completely changed the experience of owning an MP3 player. It was not the added capacity, the catchy name, or the Apple brand that turned the iPod into the most wanted music player, but rather a sharp focus on customer experience. Everything about the music player was appealing: the store, the box, the aesthetics, the white earphones, and above all, iTunes, Apple's free software that you used to manage your music. It was simple: Plug the device into the computer and the music was automatically transferred to the iPod. The product was so beautiful that it transformed a geeky piece of electronics into a piece of jewelry that everyone loved wearing. Apple iPod became successful so quickly because it added value for customers on many levels, including ease of use, abundance of features, aesthetic appeal, emotional experience, and the "cool" identity.

Back in 2001, the iPod was not as ubiquitous as we think of it being today. In its early days, Apple hardly sold any iPods. Three-hundred and ninety-nine dollars was a hefty price for a nice-to-have gadget, especially when other MP3 players hovered around $200. Apple strongly believed in the superiority of its product, but it knew that adoption would be the key to the iPod's success. During the first few months after the launch, Apple pumped more than $28 million into marketing the iPod. Some analysts estimated that every iPod sold was costing Apple nearly twice the amount it was charging. Apple devised many clever marketing techniques.

The billboards with dark silhouettes dancing with white headphones portrayed moments of ecstasy and called to the inner rebel in young people. People started buying expensive music players as symbols of identity and status. Apple kept pushing iPod until it became the standard and the MP3 player of choice.

This marketing push for adoption leads to perhaps the most important conclusion. Innovation is a combination of new and existing inventions, executed in ways that add compelling value, and customers adopting the product because they feel that the value is worth the price. Innovation has many definitions, and it means different things to different people and organizations. Without trying to redefine innovation, or create a new dictionary meaning for the word, here's my mathematical formula describing innovation:

Innovation = Ideas + Execution + Adoption

The key lesson I learned from Apple and other innovative companies is that you do not have to invent something to be innovative. Your products have to add value for customers. There are many ways to add value to products and services that already exist in the market, including the ones your company is selling. Instead of chasing wild new ideas, focus innovation efforts on adding value in new ways. Theodore Levitt, a Harvard professor and renowned market researcher, said it best in his famous quote, "Creativity is about *thinking up* new things. Innovation is *doing* new things." Instead of creating new things, do new things that will add value for your customers.

TYPES OF INNOVATIONS

In his book *The Innovator's Dilemma*, Clayton Christensen notes that innovation can be classified into two categories: disruptive innovation and sustained innovation. According to Professor Christensen, disruptive innovations introduce products or service offerings that did not exist and often help create new markets. Disruptive innovations often emerge through the use of new technologies and techniques that were previously considered unrelated or did not exist. These products are often poor in quality in the beginning and try to tap into the low end of the market. Established competitors often see little or no threat from these products. However, as the underlying technologies improve, these products improve and eventually become the new standard in the market.

Some examples of disruptive innovation include the invention of the airplane by the Wright Brothers in 1903, which was initially seen as an expensive curiosity. It took nearly fifteen years before the airplane was accepted as a viable mode of transportation and weapon of war. Similarly, when transistor radios came to the market in the early 1960s, their quality was very poor compared to existing tube-based radios. However, they were very portable. Consumers traded quality for portability. Eventually, as semiconductor technology improved, so did transistor radios, ultimately killing tube technology altogether. The transistor radio was a disruptive innovation, which served an underserved market, especially teens who wanted to listen to music away from their parents, and its portability appealed to a whole new market of people who loved taking their music with them as they moved around.

Disruptive innovations create breakthrough products and get a lot of media attention, so we naturally gravitate toward disruptive innovation. But you don't have to invent breakthrough, brand new products in order to be innovative. Innovation is about creating value, and you can add value for existing customers in ways that increase your market share. Using new techniques to add value to existing products is called incremental or sustained innovation. Disruptive innovation creates more buzz, but sustained innovation often adds more to bottom-line profits. Sustained innovations are also less risky, and you don't need to devise new business models to penetrate new market segments.

Toyota is a good example of sustained innovation. As we discussed in Chapter One, Toyota did not invent the car, but it perfected the process of car manufacturing. Toyota introduced measures to improve quality at every step of the process and required its suppliers to embrace the same approach. It empowered its line level employees to make suggestions to improve manufacturing processes and minimize faults. Toyota built cost-effective, yet very high quality cars, which allowed it to surpass U.S. automakers and dominate the global market.

Sustained innovation does not trigger the "wow" factor, so our society does not always value sustained innovation as much as disruptive innovation. Sustained innovation does not have sudden, big payoffs like disruptive innovation. However, sustained innovation is very important to staying competitive and funding future disruptive innovations. Additionally, if you are in a service industry or certain markets where you cannot develop disruptive innovations as frequently as the consumer products industry can, then sustained innovation is your only option. One can argue that all companies work continuously to improve their products. If they don't, they will perish. It is very difficult to find a successful company that does not invest in improving its processes and products, but the difference lies in how the company goes about making these improvements. A formal innovation program focused on driving sustained innovation puts the need for improvements on steroids and embeds innovation into the DNA of the company. It makes continuous improvements a habit and opens the door for disruptive innovations.

Even for companies that engage in disruptive innovation, improving existing products through sustained innovation is a no brainer. They can supplement their disruptive innovations with sustained innovation to create market dominance. They can take their successful products and create focused efforts to lower cost, add product features, and improve other life cycle aspects like manufacturing, selling, and servicing, to reach an even broader market. They can leverage technological advancements to improve business processes or enhance customer experience. This philosophy is at the heart of Apple's business model, and you can see it in the evolution of all of its products.

Do not wait for that genius product idea; start enhancing the products or services you have now. I am sure you already have a few ideas up your sleeve to enhance your products. If not, ask around on your floor. I guarantee you that there are many employees who do. Perhaps that is our gateway into another segment of the innovation journey. You don't have to bear the burden of generating all the ideas needed to grow your business. You can outsource idea generation to a number of different sources, including your employees, partners, customers, stakeholders, and even complete strangers.

Most companies fail to innovate because they are not receptive to the idea that enhancing existing products is innovative. The grass always looks greener on the other side. They cling to the notion of developing new products, which often end up costing companies more money than the new revenues they generate. This belief is further engrained in their minds by the notion that innovative ideas emerge in full form with "success" written all over them. In reality, this notion could not be farther from the truth. It is rarely the case that a single idea made a company successful. Most people attribute Google's success to its search capabilities. Contrary to popular belief, it was not the search algorithm that made Google so successful. Google tried to sell its search engine for $2 million, but nobody wanted to buy it. Google licensed its search service to AOL, Yahoo, and other big names to pay the bills. It was only after Google integrated a seemingly mundane ad engine into the search results that Google started to show some signs of potential. Similarly, what was Zappos' genius idea—selling shoes online? Not really. How Zappos serves its customers is what sets it apart from the competition. It is the execution of hundreds of ideas adding value through excellent service and a very lean fulfillment operation. The examples are countless, and we will explore many more throughout this book.

All products start from a very simple idea, and the successful products morph into outstanding innovations through continuous incremental improvements. While many slow-lane companies opt for an attitude of "If it ain't broke, don't fix it," innovative companies continuously keep looking for ways to add value and provide a better experience through service. Successful innovators keep out-innovating their own products before the competition does. Steve Jobs always worried about which product could potentially eat into the iPod market. That concern was the number one reason why he pushed to develop the iPhone. Cell phones already had the needed technology to play music, and he knew that consumers would eventually gravitate toward buying a phone with a music player, rather than carrying two devices. Apple realized that if it did not enter the cell phone market, a phone company would steal the iPod's market share. The idea of the iPad tablet was conceived before the iPhone, but Steve Jobs realized the threat from emerging cell phones and tabled the iPad idea to develop the iPhone. Again, Apple did not invent the touchscreen phone with Internet capabilities, but rather looked for ways to add value just as it had done for the iPod.

Hopefully by now, I have convinced you that you don't have to invent new products to be innovative. You can be innovative by adding value through existing products and services. In the next chapter, we will discuss the business areas where innovation can happen.

RECAP

- Most people associate innovation with invention; however, you don't need to invent something to be innovative.

- Innovation is about executing new and old ideas in ways that add value for customers and the company.

- Common techniques to add value include: speed, simplicity, convenience, lower cost, new features, aesthetics, experience, and emotional appeal.

- Disruptive innovations create new, breakthrough products that didn't exist before, while sustained innovation adds value by enhancing existing products and services.

- Ideas rarely emerge fully formed—what appears to be a novel idea is often a collection of several ideas.

- Innovative companies improve their products constantly to out-innovate themselves before the competition does.

Chapter Two Exercises

Q1. What are the top five innovative companies you admire?

1. _____

2. _____

3. _____

4. _____

5. _____

Q2. Out of these five, how many of them actually invented the product or service that made them successful?

_____

_____

_____

Q3. For each of these five companies, can you list at least three or more qualities that make them so innovative?

1. _____

2. _____

3. _____

4. _____

5. _____

Q4. Of the qualities you listed above, which five qualities can you bring to your company, or improve on to deliver stronger customer value?

1. _____

2. _____

3. _____

4. _____

5. _____

Chapter 3

Thinking Beyond Products

He who adapts fastest wins.
— Sun Tzu

It is never any one thing that makes a company innovative or successful. For Apple, it was not the MP3 player; for Google, it was not the search engine; for P&G, it was not any one consumer product; for Amazon, it was not selling books online, and for Starbucks, it was not selling expensive coffee. All of these products had existed well before these companies ventured into these domains. It is always a series of things companies do that add such compelling value that customers switch their buying habits to try these new products. These companies innovate on multiple levels, which makes them stand out from the competition, and by the time the competition notices their advances or has had time to copy their models, the innovative companies move on to the next level of value adds. They continuously experiment to discover what works and what doesn't, they learn from their mistakes, and they change course quickly to respond to market needs.

Creating breakthrough products is the most commonly assumed form of innovation. Launching new and improved products every year has been the key strategy for Apple and it has served Apple well. However, innovation does not have to be limited to developing new products. Amazon, eBay, and Netflix did not thrive by creating new products, but rather changing the business model by which they serve customers. I remember very vividly when Borders Bookstore wanted to open a new store in the Haight-Ashbury neighborhood of San Francisco. People protested that such a store would kill the neighborhood bookstores, coffee shops, and the whole neighborhood along with it. Perhaps these feelings were best captured in the 1998 movie *You've Got Mail*. Yes, it is true; Borders was taking over and wiping out many corner bookstores. Or at least so it seemed.

But then along came a true innovator: Amazon. The rest is history. Today, Borders is no more. And only a few neighborhood bookstores survive. Companies like eBay and Amazon took advantage of the new technology—the Internet—and developed business models to sell products on the Internet that had been sold through physical stores for decades. The logic behind Amazon's business model was the idea that many consumers do not physically need to inspect or handle a product that they want to buy. Books are not mysterious items. If you want to buy the latest Harry Potter novel, you do not need to see it or touch it before you buy it. You can see the cover design and even read a sample of it on Amazon. That's enough information to make you feel comfortable about plunking down fifteen dollars for a book that would cost you twenty at your local bookstore. But it was not the idea of selling books online that made Amazon an over $100 billion company; rather it was its relentless pursuit for new markets and new revenues.

Most innovative companies have one thing they do really well, while keeping a tight rein on other aspects of the business. Doing one thing well also helps to create an organizational focus as a company becomes larger. Then, the core corporate strategies and organizational culture are optimized to serve one dominant domain. For example, Southwest Airlines has a strong focus on cost savings. When making business decisions, Southwest will evaluate all decisions against that focus. For example, free lunch might increase customer loyalty, but it will also increase the cost, so Southwest does not serve lunches. Celebrating customers' birthdays creates an atmosphere of fun and surely beats the trapped travel boredom, but you cannot throw confetti since it will increase cleaning costs and create delays in plane turnaround time. Instead, Southwest employees are free to use their singing talent to entertain passengers. Southwest might be pinching pennies at every cost point, but it also has a strong customer service focus. Southwest is on a constant hunt for ideas that will help it lower costs, while still providing good service. This focus ensures that all employees are thinking of ways to improve service and operations, but under an overarching theme of lowering cost. While Southwest's focus is cost savings, Apple is focused on generating new revenue through new products. These areas of focus for innovation can be broadly classified into four business domains:

- Revenue Generation
- Cost Reduction
- Business Process
- Business Model

Let's look at these four business domains in detail.

REVENUE GENERATION

The revenue-generating domain of innovation pertains to ideas that contribute to top-line growth. This focus is the most obvious for many organizations, and under this focus, creating new products is the most prevalent strategy. Apple has done a fine job in creating new demand by releasing new products every year. It is amazing how every year people sell their old iPads on eBay and stand in line to buy the new one. It is a great strategy. It not only meets the needs of high-end-technology-hungry consumers, but also satisfies the price-sensitive consumers who are happy with the good-enough-last-year's model. Every company is interested in growth and generating new revenues. However, this organic growth focus is different from having an explicit focus to be constantly hunting for new ideas to generate new revenues.

Creating new products is a great strategy, but it is simply just one of the approaches to generating new revenue. Creating new products creates new demand, but so does expanding your business to new markets. Other aspects might include bundling of products, introducing supporting services, new sales channels, new geographic territories, new market segments, or new marketing strategies. All of these approaches contribute to top-line growth. Revenue-generating ideas could be anything that contributes to top-line growth, and it is definitely not limited to new products. In addition, the new products strategy does not work for every business. The service sector makes up a large part of the U.S. GDP, but it has no physical products that can easily showcase their advancements. Additionally, there are large numbers of commodity businesses that produce the same old product for decades. These include oil, raw metals, paper, farm products, as well as ubiquitous products like paper clips and Elmer's Glue. Product improvement cycles for these products can be very long, and consumers often buy these products on price or the brand value alone.

Countless examples exist of businesses that operate in old-line sectors, but that have innovated in a number of ways to generate new revenues. Let's look at coffee, for example. When Howard Schultz was pitching his café idea to investors, the coffee industry was on a continuous decline. It was on its way to becoming another agricultural commodity. The idea of a chain of coffee shops surely did not qualify for Venture Capital money. Contrary to business analysts' view of the coffee industry and business trends, and despite being battered by many recessions, Starbucks has been the darling of Wall Street and stands tall among the most innovative companies. Many specialty coffee shops had focused on the experience and offered options to customize their drinks, but none of them had successfully managed to expand their territories. At the heart of Starbucks' success is its focus on engaging employees to be on the lookout for ideas.

Howard Schultz had a vision of bringing an authentic Italian café experience to America, so in its early days, the Starbucks menu was written in Italian, baristas wore bow ties, and the stores played constant opera music in the background. It was a fine experience, but not exactly what American consumers appreciated. Luckily, Starbucks had built a culture of listening to customers to improve its products. It took feedback from customers and continuously experimented with various customer wants and needs. Starbucks' strong customer focus paid off handsomely in a highly commoditized business. Starbucks believed in the motto that customers are always telling you what they want, and if their requests are reasonable, why not fulfill them? In Starbucks' early days, one of these requests included two percent milk instead of whole milk. These requests contradicted the early vision of the company to deliver an authentic Italian café experience, but Starbucks chose to respond to what its customers wanted. Starbucks' coffee sales shot up dramatically as soon as it let people choose which milk they preferred. Building on its earlier success with "have it your way," Starbucks went on a flavor frenzy, which became the signature specialty of Starbucks.

COST REDUCTION

As the name suggests, this domain encompasses ideas that help lower the operational costs of a business. Wal-Mart and Southwest relentlessly focus on providing value to customers through lowered cost. Therefore, ideas that help lower operational costs are given precedence over all other types of ideas.

New materials, technological advancements, and automation are perhaps the biggest contributors in this domain. The price of technology is dropping every day while the production capacity of machines is increasing. Tooling machines are more flexible than ever and the number of off-the-shelf software solutions currently available is simply overwhelming. Today, very few business functions do not have a pre-packaged solution in the market. Software and machines are so integrated and advanced that you can almost automate every part of a business and retain people only to manage exceptions. Even in the support functions, where you need a human interaction, you will find many activities that can be automated or done more efficiently with modern systems without compromising the integrity of the product or service. A number of ways exist for how you can leverage new technologies to help reduce costs or change the way products are delivered to customers. The latest trends in Cloud technologies make it possible to leverage technology without incurring the overhead of upfront software and hardware costs, and without having to dedicate resources to maintain the infrastructure and the software. You can focus your human resources on maximizing technology utilization instead of managing the technology.

One such idea we implemented under this cost-reduction directive was to deliver insurance policies electronically. We stopped mailing physical copies of customers' policies and made them available for download on our member website. If policyholders want the paper copy, they can print it or request a copy be mailed to them. We were very concerned when we implemented this change since our customers are busy executives and business owners who have many other important issues on their minds. We worried that they might not appreciate this change and view it as a hassle and extra effort on their end to access and print policies. We were ready for an onslaught of calls, but to our surprise, we received only one phone call. Instead, our policyholders and agents appreciated the fact that they could access the policy whenever they needed it, and they wouldn't have to store pieces of paper in their drawers. It turned out that many were scanning the policy documents and storing them electronically. We saved them time and the extra effort they put into scanning and storing documents. The people who did call turned out to have been using the paper copy we mailed as a reminder. Luckily, we were easily able to satisfy the needs of those customers through other means and save the company several hundred thousand dollars per year in supplies, postage, and labor to mail the beautifully designed and carefully collated policy packets. Today, this change looks like a no-brainer, but it was revolutionary at that time. This is another aspect of innovation: When you look back, you wonder why you ever did things the way you did.

Printing appears to be a miniscule activity, but you would be amazed by how much money companies spend on printing costs, as well as discarding or storing the printed materials. People print things out of habit. After one of my keynote presentations, an attendee shared his experience about how his company dramatically reduced printing costs. I don't recall the dollar value, but it was huge. Management posted signs with cost per print next to each printer. Although color laser printers are very cheap now, color printing costs can still be ten times that of black-and-white. So they posted the average cost of color and black-and-white prints. It didn't take long for employees to reduce the number of color prints. You can take this idea to the next level by mounting a picture showing how many trees it takes to produce a ream of paper. It will make everyone think twice before printing, and you will lower your printing cost even more. Many people print out of habit and often print color because it is the default option. You can change settings so employees explicitly have to select color if they need it. Additionally, reading on LCD monitors is less strenuous on your eyes than reading off bright white paper. It is a win-win for everyone. It saves your eyes and helps your company save money.

Every function in a company effects operational costs, so you will be amazed how many ideas you can generate to lower costs or eliminate certain expenses altogether. If these ideas are coming from employees, they won't feel that management is taking away their perks, but instead they will take ownership and drive adoption. I have found many instances where management was reluctant to change things, thinking it would negatively affect employee morale. Meanwhile, employees felt that management was wasting money, but said nothing out of fear. Consider training for example. Typical classroom training is expensive and forces employees to be out of the office for several days in a row. Depending on where the training is held, you may incur additional travel expenses, which in some cases might be as costly as the training itself. Now compare that with online training where employees can watch the instructional videos at their own pace, repeat them as needed, stop them before they become overwhelming, or accelerate them if needed. Additionally, employees may prefer to do the training outside of normal working hours—at night or during the weekend—for convenience and out of a personal desire not to affect their productivity.

Technology, however, is not the only means to lower costs. Cost saving ideas could be as simple as renegotiating contracts to lower prices or take advantage of bundled packages. Even companies that provide basic amenities like electricity and telephone service are constantly changing their service plans, so lowering costs might be just a matter of picking up the phone and asking whether they have any new plans that can save you money. Changing banks or shopping for lower interest rates is another example to shed huge operational expenses.

BUSINESS PROCESS

Process innovation is perhaps the most overlooked and under-appreciated domain of innovation. In my view, business processes are perhaps the most important domain to innovate—especially customer facing processes.

Business processes are defined as a set of activities that companies do in order to transform their resources into products or services of greater value to their customers. In essence, if money is the blood of the company, processes are the veins through which that money flows to provide the needed nourishment to the entire system. All employees perform their job activities under some written or adapted process. Consistency, convenience, and efficiency generated by these processes add value for customers on multiple levels. In today's economy, where products become commoditized in months, business processes are the most valuable intellectual property companies have to maintain their competitive advantage.

Business processes can be classified into three major categories:

- Customer facing processes
- Internal processes
- Partnership processes

Customer facing processes include activities that directly influence customer experience. These activities include all direct interactions like in-person meetings, phone, web, or the good old fax machine, as well as indirect activities like marketing, community involvement, brand value proposition, and other communication activities that influence customers' decisions and overall satisfaction with the brand. Internal processes represent the set of protocols employees follow to perform their jobs, use corporate systems, and collaborate with other employees. Partner processes include the activities employees perform to collaborate with outside entities that aid a company's value creation process. All business processes influence customer experience, whether directly or indirectly, and should be reviewed periodically to ensure maximum value creation. Improvement in any process adds value for customers, but customer facing processes deserve extra attention. Improvements to customer facing processes yield the highest value and should be the number one priority for all organizations.

Look at all the activities that go on inside your organization, from trying to convert a lead into a customer to then delivering the goods and services after the purchase. Evaluate each customer touchpoint, means of communication, and the steps your employees take to close a deal or serve the customer. The goal should be to make it as easy as possible for the customer to buy your product or get help when needed. On the other end, innovating internal processes improves operational efficiencies and creates value through lowered production cost. Typically, systems replacement and organizational restructuring are the most common turning points when organizations revisit internal processes changes, but these change points are very few and far between. Looking for process improvements should be an everyday habit and part of everyone's job.

Business process improvement is also the easiest domain to innovate since you have tremendous control over your processes. Employees can also easily relate to this domain since they are responsible for executing the established processes to perform their jobs and serve customers. Processes are critical for scaling the business, increasing productivity, reducing errors, transferring knowledge, and for countless other reasons. However, no processes can ever be designed to perfection. No matter how hard a process designer may try, he or she cannot anticipate every problem and build enough agility into the process to address market changes. Processes are often educated guesses, at best, based on information available at a given point in time. Business processes should be seen as guidelines to follow, and everyone in the company should be encouraged to improve or deviate from these processes as needed to increase productivity or better serve customers.

The concept of processes goes back to the early days of industrialization, and processes are still an integral part of running any business. However, with the adoption of technology and the global shift to an information-based economy, processes become obsolete faster than ever. For information workers, processes often present more challenges than efficiencies. I am not suggesting that we should get rid of processes, but rather, we should revisit these processes frequently. Employees performing the job should be allowed to deviate from the process as needed and raise concerns if the process is no longer effective.

BUSINESS MODEL

Business model innovations address the "how" part of the value proposition of a business. A business model is the overarching process of an organization and explains how it transforms the input of labor, knowledge, material, means of distribution, and other resources into a product or service that customers feel is worth the money they pay for it. Business models also address how an organization acquires and serves its customers, and, at times, how it charges its customers in exchange for the value it delivers.

Business model innovations entail changing one or more input resources in ways that deliver value to customers. Most business model innovations tend to be large, strategic initiatives, and you may not see many ideas in the business model innovations category from your employees. However, if you educate employees on your business model and how your company's business model adds value for customers, you might be surprised by how many ways you can augment your current business model.

Advancements in technology constantly challenge the way we do business. The most recent change has been the Internet and mobile technologies. The Internet created a new medium for selling goods and services. For many industries, it has completely altered the way we buy or sell goods. Netflix is a good example that everyone can relate to. Netflix took the age-old business of movie rental and changed the business model by using the Internet to rent movies. It did not invent the movie rental business or selling goods and services online. It changed the business model of how movies were rented and delivered to viewers. Netflix changed the movie rental business just as advancements in transportation and refrigeration a century ago changed the business model of the food industry.

The means of finding and reaching out to customers are constantly changing and so are customer expectations. In today's information age, business models are changing faster than ever. Business model innovation is perhaps the most difficult to execute, but it also carries the highest payoff. Often a company is reluctant to change its business model because it has been successful in the past. Trying new things appears risky to the brand, and it challenges the established processes and norms. However, failure to innovate the business model is also the number one reason why many established organizations lose their market shares to new entrants. The newspaper industry failed to innovate after the birth of the Internet and lost its market share to websites like Craigslist. If you don't adapt and change your business model with time, there is a high likelihood that you will perish.

The best way to innovate business models is to keep trying new things. You don't have to launch extravagant initiatives for business transformation, but rather small projects to keep testing the market. IKEA is a fine example of how to innovate a business model while maintaining the traditional business. Furniture has been sold for centuries, but in the past few decades, IKEA has completely changed how we view and buy furniture. IKEA took the concept of small, foldable furniture and created modular and inexpensive products, saving on storage costs as well assembly costs. For prior generations, furniture was a long-term investment, but the younger generation views furniture as temporary disposable items.

IKEA was a traditional furniture shop in Sweden until it started to manufacture easy to transport and assemble furniture. The concept of foldable furniture originated from a marketing employee's frustration when the employee couldn't load the furniture back into the truck after a photoshoot. The photographer suggested taking the legs off the table. Bingo! A new idea for transporting and assembling furniture was born. IKEA did not abandon its current market or the way it was selling furniture, but it introduced a new option to let customers assemble their own furniture for lower aesthetic value items like outdoor tables and chairs where the final finishes were not as important. It saved customers money and eliminated the delivery hassle. As the demand for self-assembly furniture grew, IKEA built a new business model around self-assembly furniture. This new business model enabled IKEA to expand its footprint worldwide. One employee's idea transformed IKEA from a local mom-and-pop shop to a global giant.

Smaller companies tend to be more nimble, and they can change direction quickly if something in their business model is not working. The lack of safeguards and the need to hang on to their limited market share pushes smaller companies to be more agile. But this does not mean that larger organizations cannot create means to test markets. Larger companies have the needed funds to try out different ideas, so they just need to make it a corporate priority to test markets. Assemble teams and foster a culture where it is okay to try new things and it is okay if ideas do not pan out.

IBM is a fine example of a large company that changed its business model of software development. Traditionally, IBM has developed various software applications in-house that ran on its proprietary hardware. By the mid-90s, IBM lost a significant portion of its market to modular hardware and software companies like Microsoft and Dell. Closely integrated systems were IBM's key advantage in the past, but IBM realized that the computer industry had become commoditized, and developing proprietary software was very expensive. IBM decided to change its approach toward software and hardware integration. IBM partnered with the Open-Source software community and started offering Open-Source software as part of its solution offerings. Like IKEA, IBM's business model change was not an overnight transformation. IBM experimented with using Open-Source software where it had little to lose. In 1998, Apache, the open-source software, had already captured more than 50 percent of the market share, while IBM's web server software, Domino, accounted for less than 1 percent of total market share. Until this point, IBM had been a closed system and IBM hardware only ran IBM software. Good luck if you wanted to integrate or use different software to take advantage of emerging technologies. A handful of IBM engineers who regularly participated in Open-Source Software communities spurred this idea of using Open-Source software on IBM hardware. Building on small successes, IBM radically changed its software development business model. Now IBM is deeply entrenched in the Open-Source community and saves more than a billion dollars a year in software development. This business model change has helped IBM regain part of its market share in both hardware and software.

Business models are the solid bedrock for most companies, but today's fast changing environment is constantly challenging these foundations. The rapidly evolving means of distribution, customer acquisition, and servicing presents both opportunities and challenges for companies. Many schools of thought exist on how to deal with these ongoing challenges. Some experts suggest that all companies should have dedicated new product development teams to test markets, while others prefer the Venture Capital model to bring outside innovations. In my view, it doesn't matter how you test markets, but rather that you make sure you are constantly testing markets. As you test markets with new ideas, your customers will give you feedback and your ideas will evolve over time. Continuous improvements and testing markets with new ideas reduce the need for major overhaul initiatives.

Understanding domains of innovation can help identify where you want to focus your idea generation efforts. Ideas are at the heart of innovation. All ideas, whether big or small, add to customer value creation. In the next chapter, we will discuss where ideas can come from and how you can create an environment to harness those ideas.

RECAP

- There are four major domains of innovation: Revenue Generating, Cost Savings, Business Process, and Business Model.

- Most people associate innovation with new products; however, creating new products is just one of the strategies under the Revenue Generating domain.

- Most innovative companies align their core competencies to one of these four domains, while keeping a close eye on the others.

- Process innovation is the most underappreciated, yet it can be the most advantageous domain of innovation.

- You can innovate and increase market share by lowering cost or creating new business models that increase market reach.

Chapter Three Exercises

Q1. What products or services does your company sell?

_____

_____

_____

_____

_____

_____

Q2. What are the top five attributes that make your products superior or give your company a competitive advantage?

_____

_____

_____

_____

_____

_____

Q3. Which innovation domains are most applicable to your business? List them in the order they make the most impact.

_____

_____

_____

_____

_____

Chapter 4

Embedding Innovation in the DNA

A pessimist sees challenge in every opportunity;
an optimist sees opportunity in each challenge.
— Winston Churchill

Innovation researchers have long agreed that there are only two drivers of innovation: top-down innovations and bottom-up innovations. Ideas can come from anywhere, but these are the only two real forces that transform ideas into innovations. Jean-Philippe Deschamps, Professor of Technology and Innovation at IMD Business School, characterizes the difference between the two as: top-down innovation is initiated by the management and supported by the employees, while the bottom-up innovation is initiated by the employees and supported by the management.

As we discussed in Chapter Two, innovation has three critical components: ideas, execution, and adoption. All three pieces must come together for a concept to morph into innovation. All ideas face capital, intellectual, technical, and political challenges. These challenges can be overcome only if management creates the focus and employees align their efforts toward that focus and find creative solutions to make the products successful. This alignment and focus can be driven by strong management directives and processes, or it can come from employees as a passion to do great things, be part of something bigger, and make contributions toward a greater cause. The successful companies leverage both to drive continuous innovation. People credit Steve Jobs for his vision and focus, but they often underestimate the emphasis he placed on having great people to drive innovation at every decision point. Steve Jobs did not invent the iPod, or the iconic navigation scroll, or the iTunes store. All of these ideas came from the bright employees he hired. Steve Jobs drove the vision of building a great portable music player, and his staff came up with ideas to turn that vision into reality.

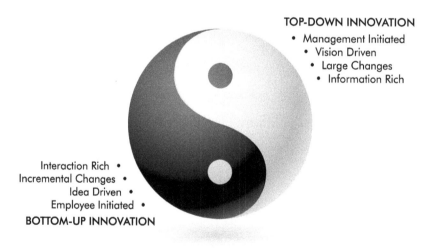

TOP-DOWN INNOVATION
- Management Initiated
- Vision Driven
- Large Changes
- Information Rich

Interaction Rich •
Incremental Changes •
Idea Driven •
Employee Initiated •
BOTTOM-UP INNOVATION

TOP-DOWN INNOVATION

Top-down innovation is often driven by vision, sudden market changes, leadership changes, or some type of disaster. Any of these changes can cause management to spring into action and develop approaches to respond to these changes. Top-down innovation is initiated by management, often as a vision or an ambitious goal, which is then translated into actionable items for the staff to carry out.

Ford's Model A, introduced in 1927, is a classic example of vision-driven top-down innovation. By the mid-1920s, the company's flagship car, the sturdy and ubiquitous Model T, had been refined, manufactured, and sold for over fifteen years. Yet competition was overtaking the old design, and it was clear that the Model T was becoming obsolete. Edsel Ford, Henry's son, wanted to build a more advanced and powerful car for the growing middle-class market. He secretly assembled a team of engineers, and within a few months, he had designed the successor to the Model T. The vast assembly lines at Ford were shut down, the lines retooled for the new car, and then the lines were reactivated to produce the Model A. The car was an immediate hit and is credited for saving the company. The Model T was a disruptive innovation and the Model A was a sustained innovation. Both models were the top-down innovation visions of the company's leaders, which played a vital role in building the Ford brand.

Top management is perhaps the most conventional source for innovation. People at the top are responsible for growing the business and meeting their customers' needs. Management is the most informed about market conditions, the competitive landscape, and company operations. Packed with this body of knowledge, management looks for ways to meet market needs, beat the competition, and add product features to grow their market share.

It is customary among mid-sized to large businesses to create annual and multi-year plans where management decides on the direction and projects to undertake at any given point. Anyone who has been involved in these planning meetings knows that this is often a mixed bag of activities; nevertheless, it is still a valid source of innovation. Top ranking managers bring their experiences and expertise to the process of coming up with new ideas to grow the business or respond to market needs. Businesses have operated under this model since the industrial revolution, and most operate this way today. There is nothing terribly wrong with this model, with the exception that the idea pool is limited to a handful of individuals. Sometimes, these individuals are so far removed from customers that all the ideas they generate are heavily company centric often at the customer's expense.

Top-down innovation has been the norm for centuries, and over the years, companies have developed many successful top-down techniques, including Research and Development, partnership, and outsourcing. It is nearly impossible not to discuss the role of research and development when talking about innovation. Research and Development, or R&D for short, is a natural extension of top-down innovation. In top-down innovation environments, it is very common for management to use R&D to develop new products and enhance existing products. When the challenge is known or driven by specific needs, R&D is the best option to drive innovation. R&D teams are tasked to solve specific challenges or create new products that meet specific needs. R&D groups are often isolated from day-to-day operations so their creativity is not hampered by daily operational logistics. Most innovative companies have some form of R&D group dedicated to developing the next generation of products or improving existing products with radical new enhancements. For companies that sell physical goods, R&D is almost a necessity in the race to stay ahead or on par with the competition. Pharmaceutical, consumer goods, and high-tech manufacturing companies are the most common examples of industries that depend on the outcome of R&D efforts to grow business, stay competitive, or create new markets.

Partnership is an alternative to R&D, where a company partners with another company to augment its domain expertise. Partnership can bring domain expertise into a new area and cut R&D time significantly. Some companies completely rely on external innovations, also known as the outside-in innovation model. They buy or borrow fully developed products, and they use their core competencies to take the products to a much broader market. Dell, for example, partners with other companies to license their research and then uses its strength in the supply chain to bring that product to market. Silicon Valley venture funding is set up around developing companies to meet the need of larger brands to outsource risky ventures to new start-up companies.

Recently, a new model of outsourcing innovation to complete strangers has been gaining momentum. Innocentive.com, which was initially started by Eli Lilly to outsource some of its most difficult scientific challenges, is the biggest success story of outsourcing innovation to strangers. Innocentive.com is now a platform where anyone can post any problem, from a very specific chemistry problem to much broader anthropology issues. All the Open-Source software products are also built by outsourcing software development to strangers. In many cases, the quality of the Open-Source software product is far superior to those developed by leading software houses.

BOTTOM-UP INNOVATION

Ideas can come from anywhere, and a front-line employee can be as important a source of ideas as top management and those in the R&D department. Encouraging all employees to develop new and innovative ideas is referred to as bottom-up innovation. Employees are involved in day-to-day operations, and they interact with the products and customers more than management does, so they can be a rich source of customer intelligence. Employees know business processes better than management, so they are an excellent source of ideas to improve company operations, increase productivity, and align products with customer desires.

Bottom-up innovation is idea driven. An employee is going about doing his normal job activities when he realizes the job he or she is trying to get done can be done differently, and perhaps more effectively. Thus, an idea is born. Management encourages employees to submit ideas and creates an environment where ideas are nurtured and celebrated. Employees submit ideas that help improve customer satisfaction, increase operational efficiencies, add product features, and improve business processes that could benefit the customer, company, or stakeholders. The ideas are developed in the open, so no ideas are squashed or lost in the process. The ideas flow upward to management for funding and implementation support. Most of the ideas generated by employees tend to be incremental in nature, but sometimes truly disruptive ideas can also emerge out of this process. Once such a culture is established, innovation becomes everyone's job and your entire workforce becomes an extension of R&D. Google, 3M, and Starbucks are a few examples of companies that leverage their entire workforces to develop new products using this approach.

Bottom-up innovation is a relatively new concept in the business world and a great deal of credit goes to 3M for paving the way. 3M is the most prominent example of a company that created a formal structure to encourage employees to generate ideas and develop new products that would help grow the business. 3M's "15 percent time" program encourages employees to allocate a portion of their paid time to experiment and work on their own ideas. While you may think of it as a costly employee benefit, for 3M, it is the lifeblood of the company. This program has produced many of the company's best-selling products, including Post-it notes. 3M pioneered the concept of dedicated experimentation time, which set an example for many of today's innovative companies, including Google and W.L. Gore.

Google is another famous example. Google allows its software developers to use 20 percent of their time to work on hobby projects or any other projects going on in the company that interest them. Some of the most profitable products have come of this 20 percent experimentation time, so it has been credited with fueling Google's unconventional success. For Google, it is a way of encouraging innovation at all levels and lets employees create things they are passionate about. This culture not only helped Google grow its top line, but it also created a buzz that attracted some of the brightest and most talented people, which then further reinforced continuous innovation and business growth.

Employees are directly engaged with customers and some of the best ideas often come from customers. Customers love to tell companies what they want, but front-line employees who interact with customers often have no incentive to pass this information up the chain of command. Often, business practices and processes deter employees from finding new solutions. Incentives and performance metrics deter employees from reporting ideas that could better serve the customers and aid business growth. More often, front-line employees are required to solve customer problems in as little time as possible to meet their daily targets. Instead of rewarding employees for their creativity in solving customer problems, employees are punished for not following the script or defined procedures. Eventually, employees become disgruntled and service standards drop.

Zappos sells shoes online. It is an Internet retailer, and most of its employees work in its call center and in order fulfillment. Contrary to standard call center practices, Zappos has no call center scripts. Employees are not required to say a specific greeting or follow procedures to serve the customer. The employees' goal is to provide excellent service, and they are empowered in every way to make the customer happy. Tony Hsieh, CEO of Zappos, encourages employees to observe their environment and customers and submit at least one idea per week that could improve the company or customer experience. Zappos is ranked among the top companies to work for, and many talented employees are willing to take a pay cut to go work for Zappos. This philosophy transformed Zappos into a $1.2 billion brand in less than ten years. Customers swear by the company's service and promote the company through word-of-mouth recommendations and blogs. Zappos believes that it doesn't need a marketing department; the entire company is in marketing.

Bottom-up innovation encourages employees to listen to customers and observe their environment to come up with ideas to improve the products that can benefit the company or customers. Employees feel they have a voice, and management appreciates their input. They feel like part of the company and take pride in their work. Instead of complaining about their frustrations or getting demotivated by the obstacles, they think of ways to eliminate them or get around them. Bottom-up innovation is also an excellent starting point for companies that do not have extra funds for dedicated R&D efforts. You don't need upfront capital investment to get started. As a matter of fact, I started this program when I was cutting costs. Instead of investing money, we were shrinking funds. When I needed money to implement an idea, the ideas that were worth doing justified their own funding. Besides, you will be surprised by how much low hanging fruit you can pick. We did some of our best and most exciting work during this cost-cutting period. These projects not only helped make a difference to the company's bottom line, but they also helped me retain my staff when they were most vulnerable.

Most companies are run with a belief that top management is responsible for product direction, enhancements, and process improvements. When management feels external pressure, it imposes various top-down initiatives to make process and product enhancements. Then, as market information and results slowly make their way back up to the top of the organization, executives notice inefficiencies and challenges in keeping up with the competition. They then conclude that something dramatic must be done to inject competiveness into the organization. These realizations then result in new initiatives like technology enhancements, corporate training, and organizational restructuring. While these initiatives can be very important, they often fail to yield the desired effect on corporate productivity and financial results. Often, top-down initiatives run against the tide. Employees are rarely excited about these projects and resist such initiatives. Top management feels the pressure to change, but employees have no reason to change. They are not part of the change and feel removed from corporate performance. The gap between management intent and execution grows even more.

Contrary to the top-down approach, if you *ask* employees for ideas, show them how their work makes a difference in the company, and make them feel that their ideas are welcomed, they will find creative ways to solve problems. They will work relentlessly to enhance the product to meet new requirements or market standards. This approach will increase employee engagement, which will in turn create peer pressure on laggards to perform. Engaged employees will also be more in tune with customers and the market. They will listen to customers for ideas and develop features that customers want. They will bring ideas from other industries and their own day-to-day experiences as consumers of various products and services. In addition, every company has driven employees. Some of them have big entrepreneurial dreams. Rather than having these employees work in secrecy at night or on weekends, you can tap into their desire to do something big. These employees will not only submit ideas, but they will also work with all the affected parties to see their ideas implemented. Employees see these projects as a reflection of their talent and skills, and they go the extra mile to see them succeed. It is a matter of pride and people work extra hard when their pride is involved.

A good organization is a mix of both top-down and bottom-up innovation. Top-down innovations are very important for dreaming big. Without top-down innovation, we would have never set foot on the moon, built the personal computer, or promoted personalized healthcare. It is the job of visionary leaders to push boundaries and constantly disrupt the market with new and innovative ways to add value for customers. However, leaders cannot be involved in every activity that goes on inside an organization. As the company grows, the only way to succeed is through delegation. The question then becomes: Are the delegates engaged at the same level as the leaders? Is their intent, energy, and focus aligned toward the same vision? Do they feel like part of that vision? Do they see themselves as an important piece of the puzzle in bringing that vision to reality?

Creating a bottom-up innovation program can also be instrumental in bridging the gap between strategic intent and execution. When employees are more engaged, they provide superior service to customers and come up with ideas from a very diverse perspective that often gets missed in a top-down view. In the next chapter, we will discuss how bottom-up innovation plays an even bigger role in the Service Industry.

RECAP

- There are only two real sources of innovation: top-down innovation and bottom-up innovation.

- Top-down innovation is vision-driven and initiated by management, while bottom-up innovation is idea-driven and initiated by employees.

- R&D, acquisitions, and outsourcing innovations are simply the means of achieving top-down innovations.

- Bottom-up innovation fosters a culture that encourages employees to submit ideas that add value for customers, company, and stakeholders.

- Top-down innovation is needed to drive big visions, while bottom-up innovation is vital in creating products that are aligned with customers' needs and wants.

Chapter Four Exercises

Q1. What are the top five innovative products, features, or services your company developed in the last two years?

1. _____

2. _____

3. _____

4. _____

5. _____

Q2. Can you list ten ideas that employees suggested in the last two years that directly or indirectly added value to the company or for customers?

1. _____

2. _____

3. _____

4. _____

5. _____

6. _____

7. _____

8. _____

9. _____

10. _____

Chapter 5

Innovating the Service

Don't open a shop unless you know how to smile.
— Jewish Proverb

As I started my journey of innovation, I found that Service Industries have been largely neglected by most innovation experts and authors. A lot of books have been written on product innovation that teach how to develop new products, how to create prototypes, how to test markets, and how to build demand for novel products, but very limited literature exists on how to innovate in the Service Industry. According to the U.S. Department of Commerce, service industries account for more than 79 percent of the U.S. GDP. Worldwide service industries account for 60 percent of Global GDP. The Service Industry is the largest and fastest growing sector worldwide. Even with companies that are heavily product-focused, service accounts for a large portion of their revenue and brand value.

The Service Industry is full of opportunities. We live in the Information Age, and the rise of social media has empowered customers to punish poor service providers and reward good ones. Social media presents new challenges and opportunities for service providers. If you have something unique to offer, and have high service standards, customers shower you with loyalty and referral business. When your services fall short of the competition, the same thing happens in reverse—the word spreads faster than your marketing department can react.

The word "innovation" is commonly associated with gadgets. People think of innovation in terms of the latest electronics, advancements in the automobile industry, renewable energy, robotics, or composite materials. In other words: products. It's very rare to hear someone talk about innovative service. Perhaps it's due to its very nature—service is hard to see, and it is subject to one's interpretation and expectations. Given the market share of the service sector, and the declining service standards in many advanced countries, it is safe to conclude that the service sector needs innovation more than the manufacturing sector. Given today's service standards, I feel you don't even have to innovate anything—just be nice to customers and you will win their loyalty! A little bit of empathy can go a long way.

Service is defined as an economic activity that does not result in the ownership of physical goods. The service sectors include education, financial services, healthcare, utilities, telecommunication, trade, and transportation. The end product of a service industry is a promise that cannot be seen, touched, or felt through any of our external senses.

Service is a promise. How do you innovate a promise?

People take an enormous risk when they buy a service. There is no shiny red Porsche that speaks for its quality or a fancy iPhone that conveys its status. People are always concerned that the service provider will charge them more or may not deliver the best service for the money. Customers make service purchasing decisions based on intuitive judgments and the comfort level they develop based on the information they have collected from various influencers. These influencers include brand value, rating agencies, peer reviews, and referrals. Even the small stuff, like the color of the brochure and location of the business, influences buying decisions.

Service innovation is different from physical products innovation in the sense that people look more to external influencers to judge your product than the product itself. Service innovation is challenging because you have to factor in these external influencers, but at the same time, it is easier to innovate a service because the essence of the service is simply its quality. And the quality of your service is something you can control. Products, on the other hand, can be easily copied, but copying service quality is not an easy feat.

How does your service quality stand relative to customer expectations? How do the external influencers rate your service? Are you providing the service your customers really care about? Are you serving them the way they want to be served? And, perhaps the most important question is: Are your employees delivering the level of service you are promising?

The down side of an emphasis on quality is always the cost. When it comes to service, people are often willing to pay more for high quality. But there is a limit to how much more customers will be willing to pay for higher quality service. So you cannot just throw resources at the problem. Adding resources will increase the cost of your service, and at some point, the cost will outweigh the value. Think about when you need a haircut—do you look for the cheapest hair stylist or the one you trust will do a good job? How much more are you willing to pay for that? And at what point will you say, "No, I won't pay that much for a haircut"? To improve quality without increasing cost, you need to be creative and find innovative ways to deliver service that reduces cost but improves service.

Dig deeper into who are your customers and prospects and how they like to be served. Are there service areas and interactions that you can *eliminate*, and are there areas where you can *enrich* customer interaction? As part of the promise, a service company may provide a set of services and customers may value some of those services over others. For example, if you're an auto insurance company, a customer may contact you to buy insurance, request an address change, pay dues, or file a claim. The true service a car insurance company sells is a promise to take care of the customer's car if he or she gets into an accident. But customers don't plan to get into accidents when they are buying insurance. Instead, they often think that they are good drivers and will not get into accidents. Even though your insurance company may have the best accident coverage, the customer's buying decision and rating of your service is more influenced by the convenience of buying services than the breadth of the accident coverage you provide. The focus then should go to convenience and speeding up the buying process through automation. On the other hand, when someone gets in an accident, he is emotionally shaken and may need more emotional support than the efficiencies that an automated system can provide. Using this example, you can easily interpret how a company can shift its human resources from one function to another.

To innovate in the service industry, you constantly have to ask customers what services they value the most, and how those preferences change under different circumstances. A number of techniques are available to figure out what your customers want. The most common approach is to conduct customer surveys, either with internal resources or using third party services to interview customers to help you figure out what services they value. Are there any services your customer would prefer to do for herself, any services she doesn't value at all, and times when she would prefer someone holding her hand and walking her through the process? In the Service Industry, no substitute exists for asking customers what they want. There is always the possibility that your customers might lead you along the wrong path. Customers often give feedback based on their personal experiences with you or your competitors. Going back to the auto insurance example, customer feedback might be based on the fact that the customer hasn't had an accident in ten years or out of frustration that his premium is too high because of an accident two years ago. Customer surveys can also be very expensive. To add to that, it's rare that you will have all the right questions to ask at the first attempt. Each survey will yield new insights that will cause you to ask more questions or refine the questions to make sure your customers really understand your intentions. This process may take many iterations and require outside experts. To get around the limitation of your customers' limited view of the world, you have to collect data on a large scale and combine it with your own knowledge of the business and industry.

Training employees to listen to customers, on the other hand, can be a comprehensive and relatively inexpensive tool for gathering customer intelligence. You can train your employees to listen to customers for ideas and pay attention to why customers are calling. Are they expressing frustration that they had to call you for something, or are they delighted to have found someone who can really help them? Employees can be more inquisitive when interacting with customers. Ritz-Carlton has built a reputation for excellent service by using this model. It has systematically built customer intelligence gathering at all employee levels into the company's DNA. All employees are trained to observe customers and fill out an incident report, just like the Bright Idea Box program discussed in this book. The incident report may get triggered by your stated preference for amenities or by the hotel maid noticing that you emptied five cans of Diet Coke. This information goes into a central system so the next time you are staying at the Ritz, whether in San Francisco or Shanghai, the staff will automatically try to accommodate your preferences—you'll find extra cans of Diet Coke without even asking for them.

Engaging employees in the company's core strategy gives meaning to their work, and employees are more engaged when they feel that their work contributes to the company's success. Engaged employees provide better service. Once again, the Service Industry has no physical product to remind customers of what they paid for; therefore, customers often look to interactions with the service provider to justify the service's cost. These interactions includes all the possible touchpoints that bring your name to the customer's mind. However, direct interaction with the employees who deliver that promise outweigh all other touchpoints. A good interaction with the company brings the needed reassurance that the company stands behind its promise. On the other hand, when customers interact with disengaged employees, no amount of strategy or sophistication can help sustain the business. You can have the best intentions, ambitious goals, and the grandest vision, but if your workforce is not aligned behind you, your services are destined to fail. The alignment of vision and execution is important for all business, but it is particularly important for the Service Industry. As the common saying goes, culture trumps strategy.

Asking employees to be on the lookout for customer wants and needs is neither new nor rare, but very few have understood its power. Those who have adopted this practice have radically transformed their businesses. Ritz-Carlton, Starbucks, Whole Foods, and Zappos are a few examples of companies that leverage the power of employee engagement so they can continuously innovate and lead their respective industries.

Hopefully, by now I have convinced you that regardless of whether you are a product company or a service company, you can benefit greatly from engaging employees in the idea generation process. For service industries, this type of program can do wonders. In the next section, we will discuss the details of creating the Bright Idea Box innovation program that encourages employees to submit and develop ideas.

RECAP

- The Service Industry sells a promise. It cannot be seen, touched, or felt through any of our senses.

- Customers take a risk every time they buy a service and look to external influencers for validation of their purchase.

- Service companies rely on their employees to deliver the service they promised to customers.

- Employees are a great source of customer insight. They are often more in contact with customers than management.

- Customers are always telling you what they want. Train your employees to listen to customers and come up with ideas to address those needs.

Chapter Five Exercises

Q1. What services does your company offer—all the way from the services your company sells to the mundane support activities like change of address requests?

_____

_____

_____

_____

_____

_____

Q2. What are the top five service elements that your customers value when shopping for the products and services your company sells?

1. _____

2. _____

3. _____

4. _____

5. _____

Q3. Who are the external influencers that your customers use to benchmark your service standards?

_____

_____

_____

_____

- Part Two -
THE PROGRAM

The Six-Step MASTER
Innovation Program

In the following chapters, I'll introduce the Six-Step M.A.S.T.E.R. Innovation Program. Here are the steps:

STEP 1:   Mobilize
STEP 2:   Amass
STEP 3:   Support
STEP 4:   Triage
STEP 5:   Execute
STEP 6:   Recognize

Let's look at them in detail.

Chapter 6

Step 1: Mobilize
Marching with Purpose

It is not enough to be industrious; so are the ants.
What are you industrious about?
— Henry David Thoreau

The first step in creating the Bright Idea Box program is to define and document the program's vision and purpose. A clearly defined purpose statement will help ensure the entire workforce is marching in the same direction. The purpose statement should be a working document that captures the program's essence, how it works, and the types of ideas you are seeking. It should be a three-part document outlining the purpose, objectives, and guidelines.

This purpose statement is the overarching and simplified vision of the program that serves as a guiding beacon for employees who are thinking of new ideas, as well as those responsible for supporting and ensuring that valid ideas get implemented in a timely manner. To craft a good purpose statement, you need to answer the following questions: Why do you want to create this program? How will it add value for the company and your customers? How will it add value for employees? What kinds of ideas are you expecting from employees? Are you trying to solve specific problems, exploit opportunities, or respond to changing market dynamics? Are you trying to develop new products or enhance existing products and services? The answers to these questions will also dictate your objective, guidelines, tools, and processes.

The program's primary objective is to engage employees in the process of improving company products, operations, services, and all the projects the company undertakes to fulfill its larger mission. For a variety of reasons, a strong "Us vs. Them" feeling exists among employees and management. Management may feel that employees are lazy, don't want to grow, want to do the minimum, and therefore, need to be tightly managed and pushed to do more. Employees, on the other hand, may feel that management is out to suck their blood and get rich at their expense. The program's primary goal is to eliminate this toxic feeling by inviting employees to be part of the company's success and be recognized for their contributions. Employees are intelligent human beings who are capable of solving complex business problems. They already know quite a bit about the business, and they can easily learn the new skills needed to develop ideas and improve company performance.

Creating such a program lifts the mental level of all employees from clock-punchers to partners. The program creates a sense of ownership among employees. Brasilata calls its employees "inventors" and makes them sign an "Innovator Contract," which challenges employees to be on the lookout for ideas to create better products, improve processes, and cut costs wherever possible. Brasilata gave its employees the new identity of "inventors," and employees wear this identity with pride. This made-up identity transforms the average employee, who otherwise may have never invented anything in his or her life, into an innovator capable of inventing new products and processes. This newly formed identity among employees, and the desire to live up to it, pushed Brasilata into the top twenty innovators in Brazil, according to change management experts Dan and Chip Heath. By implementing the Bright Idea Box program, you will also be creating an "innovator" identity for your employees, which will induce new ways of thinking about and doing their jobs. You probably already have employees who are highly engaged, who regularly do things to make the company more successful. This program will reward those employees and encourage others to follow their lead.

The second part of the document should outline the area of focus and the program's business objectives. The program's objectives should be closely aligned with business goals and values. If growth is the company's primary focus, then growth should be the central theme of the innovation program. If the focus is to improve customer service, then make that be an overarching theme. You need to pick domains that are most applicable to your business or the kinds of ideas you want your employees to submit. In Chapter Three, we discussed the four domains of innovation. List the business domains and business problems upon which you want your employees to focus their energy. You can use these four domains as is or you can elevate the level of a sub-domain to the top domains. For example, you may feel that you don't want employees to be thinking of new business models, but customer service needs more attention, so simply substitute Business Model with Customer Service. This list does not have to be limited to a certain number. You can expand or reduce the items as you see fit, based on your business needs and comfort level. It is also perfectly reasonable to restrict the scope of this program to operational efficiencies, so you can test the waters and train employees on the new way of thinking under a narrowly defined scope. Regardless of what you put in this list, make sure that your employees are able to translate these items to their day-to-day activities. Be as explicit as possible and avoid using fancy business buzz words that only MBA graduates or Wall Street analysts can understand. The goal is not to make the program look good on paper, but rather to create a program that employees can easily understand.

When I launched our program, my goal was to seek ideas to grow the business, lower costs, improve operational efficiencies, increase customer satisfaction, and train employees to listen to customers for ideas. I educated employees on all four major domains of innovation, but I made it clear that I was not seeking new product ideas; nor did I expect the business model to change any time soon. That said, if employees had ideas, they were welcome to submit them and the committee would pass those ideas to the appropriate business functions. Over time, we kept adding new areas and specific challenges. The most recent addition was "ideas for mobile-app features." Surprisingly, narrow and deep focus generates more ideas than a blank canvas. In the early days of your program, list explicit business challenges and opportunities as much as possible.

The objectives section also needs to outline a clear definition of what constitutes an idea. You don't want random opinions, emotional outbursts, and self-serving ideas. Along with guidelines on what kinds of ideas you want, you also need to educate employees on what differentiates an idea from an opinion.

Ideas often evolve in three stages: opinion, suggestion, and then idea.

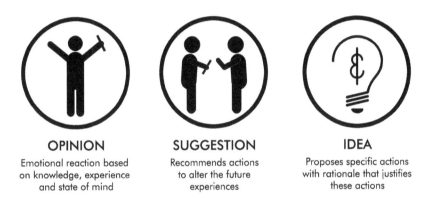

OPINION
Emotional reaction based on knowledge, experience and state of mind

SUGGESTION
Recommends actions to alter the future experiences

IDEA
Proposes specific actions with rationale that justifies these actions

Birth of an Idea: From Opinion to an Idea

Almost all ideas start from an opinion. But, as we all know, opinions are not always rational or fully thought through. They are someone's point of view based on that person's knowledge, awareness, and experience. We all form opinions when we experience frustration, learn something new, want to make a point, or desire a certain outcome. I am sure you would agree that there is no shortage of opinions. Everyone on the planet has opinions. Opinions have a bad reputation, but opinions can be very valuable if you know how to handle them. Opinions become valuable when they offer some constructive suggestions. Instead of pointing out a weakness and expressing frustration, a valuable opinion offers constructive input to make something better. PIXAR is famous for using this technique to produce very high quality animation. It even has a name for this process: Plussing. All team members gather in the morning to showcase their work and offer each other constructive input to help improve the work by "plussing" it with ideas. They don't criticize the quality of the work, but rather, they offer specific pointers to improve the scene or action. It is then up to the animator to filter that information and adapt the suggestions that make the most sense.

A suggestion throws the ball into someone else's court, and its value is often limited by the critic's own knowledge and judgment. There is no guarantee that the suggestion is any good. However, when you inject credibility and rationale behind a suggestion, it becomes an idea. In essence, an idea is an opinion that suggests constructive actions along with the rationale of why these actions make sense. So when you ask employees to submit ideas, you want to make it clear that you want ideas, not opinions. It is not always easy for employees to form the rationale, but it is important that an employee puts an effort into making the idea credible. The rationale is not a business plan or financial forecast; instead, it is a simple, thoughtful exercise that adds weight to the idea.

Your employees have opinions; the essence of the Bright Idea Box program is to convert those opinions into ideas. While it is true that employee opinions can be farfetched, inconsiderate, and some may have no bearing on reality, there is an upside to opinions; all ideas start from an opinion. It is your job to teach your employees how to transform opinions into suggestions and ideas. Don't let those opinions go to waste. Put some thought into them and convert them into suggestions. Suggestions are synonymous with constructive feedback. If the parties involved agree that the suggestion can add value to the company, it has the potential for triggering action. The next step is to take those suggested actions and make an educated guess as to the cost of the actions and the value they might bring. If the value outweighs the cost: Voila! You have an idea.

If you wish, in the objectives section you can also set goals for the idea count or financial outcomes you desire. My recommendation is to focus on the quality of ideas, rather than the quantity, but you might find some compelling benchmarks and measurements that encourage progress without compromising the quality and integrity of ideas. Keep in mind that it will take time before this kind of program becomes an integral part of your company, so setting goals could also discourage ideas or promote the wrong practices rather than eliciting more ideas.

I want to bring to your attention that this type of program is not very effective for new product development in the traditional sense, in which management is trying to launch a new product by a certain date. However, that does not mean that new products cannot emerge from this process. After all, Google Maps, Google News, Gmail, Google Docs, and many other successful products that Google launched are the outcome of their bottom-up innovation program. However, you cannot intentionally create a new product through this process. Most of the new products that emerge out of this process are more the result of serendipity than deliberate effort. These ideas often emerge from an employee's passion for something or reflect something new the employee has learned and wants to test. In the process, the employee discovers that his or her idea could add value to the company. The product development phase is much slower, iterative, and evolves through much trial and error. There is no guarantee that an idea will mature to become a market ready product or that the market will accept it. But the process is very educational for employees. When someone does stumble across a good idea, the entire team brings its valuable expertise together to making the product successful. This is why Google gives all of its employees 20 percent time to experiment—so they learn and grow, and at the same time, create a large pool of ideas.

The last section of the purpose document should outline the guidelines for participating in the program. In this section, you can include what and who is outside the scope of this program. For example, we do not accept ideas that do not add direct value to the company or customer. Participating in charity events or company outings are great team-building activities, and they add value in indirect ways, but we chose to exclude all ideas of this nature because they do not directly add value for customers. We also excluded all senior management staff from submitting ideas. Ideas submitted by top-management can intimidate employees who may not have the knowledge or background to think of grand ideas, and thus, they shy away from submitting their relatively small incremental improvement ideas. Managers have many other means of implementing their ideas and do not need such an idea program to give them a voice. The program's purpose is to increase employee involvement; therefore, only employees and line-level managers are allowed to submit ideas. If a senior management member has an idea, he or she can pass it to one of the employees. This restriction helps maintain the program's purity, and ideas are treated as ideas and not directives.

Once you have your vision and focus well-documented, you need a system for employees to submit ideas. In the next chapter, we will discuss how to select the right tool for capturing ideas.

RECAP

- Create a mission and purpose document that clearly states the desired outcome of the program.

- List business domain challenges, needs, and opportunities to define areas for employees to focus their energy.

- In the master document, detail the process flow from submitting ideas to reviewing, prioritizing, and implementing.

- All ideas originate from opinions based on knowledge, awareness, and experience.

- Educate employees on how to transform their opinions into suggestions and ideas.

- Valuable ideas suggest specific actions to benefit the company, create value propositions for customers, and identify return on investment.

Chapter Six Exercises

Q1. What benefits can your company gain from creating a Bright Idea Box program?

_____

_____

_____

_____

_____

_____

Q2. What are your top three objectives in creating this program?

_____

_____

_____

_____

_____

Q3. Keeping in mind the answers to questions one and two, can you create a very simple, one or two line vision statement for the program?

_____

_____

_____

_____

_____

_____

Q4. On which business domains, challenges, opportunities, or business functions would you like to focus?

_____

_____

_____

_____

_____

Q5. Who is allowed to submit ideas?

_____

_____

_____

Q6. Is it an internal use only program, or are there any external entities that are allowed to participate?

_____

_____

_____

Q7. Who is excluded from participating in the program?

_____

_____

_____

Chapter 7

Step 2: Amass Collecting Ideas

Words are, of course, the most powerful
drug used by mankind.
— Rudyard Kipling

The next step in building the Bright Idea Box program is creating the means for capturing ideas. Humans have infinite creative potential and we are full of ideas. The famous writer Stephen King perhaps said it the best: "There is no Idea Dump, no Story Central, no Island of the Buried Bestsellers; good story ideas seem to come quite literally from nowhere, sailing at you right out of the empty sky: two previously unrelated ideas come together and make something new under the sun. Your job isn't to find these ideas but to recognize them when they show up." Your employees have ideas, and often these ideas come and go. They get lost in the rush of activities because they are not captured and developed. You don't need to find these ideas, but rather, to create means to capture and organize these ideas when they show up. We are idea machines, but, sadly, many of our ideas get lost because we have a million other things to do, remember, and prioritize. Employees get ideas as they are going about doing their daily jobs or solving customer problems. They get ideas that would help to prevent the customers from experiencing the same frustration again. Unfortunately, employees have no systematic means for capturing those ideas or proposing alternatives beyond their scope of capability or authority. Many breakthrough ideas fall through the cracks because the company doesn't have means to capture them. For this reason, at the heart of this program is an easy to use and easy to access Idea-Capturing System, which is available to all employees to submit ideas when they are fresh in their minds.

Thankfully, there are many off-the-shelf idea-capturing products already available in the market to serve this purpose. While pre-packaged solutions do make this step very easy, that does not mean this step is any less important or deserves any less attention. This tool is very important, so you need to put some thought into selecting and configuring it. The tool plays a vital role in the program's adoption and success. It will act as a silent marketing tool that will invite employees to submit ideas, showcase existing ideas, and provide visibility into the process and evolution of ideas. This chapter is all about how to select the right tool and what features to look for in an Idea-Capturing System.

If most of your employees spend a fair amount time in front of the computer, then the obvious choice is a software solution that employees can easily access from their computers. Web-based solutions are an ideal fit for this type of program since employees can access the system from anywhere to submit and review ideas. Most of the vendors in this space offer cloud solutions, which makes access and administration even easier. If your employees don't use a computer to perform part of their job functions, you may have to look into kiosk solutions. Toyota installed kiosks throughout the plant to make it easier for assembly line employees to submit ideas. These kiosks are simply terminals integrated into the central idea-capturing software solutions.

As I'll discuss later, these idea-capturing solutions offer tremendous flexibility to customize the look, feel, and building process for evaluating and implementing ideas. But before diving deeper into the tool selection process, you need to determine what information you want to capture when employees submit ideas.

IDEA BLUEPRINT

Stanford Research Institute (SRI) is known for its pioneering research and has produced many groundbreaking commercial applications in medical devices, drug development, technology, robotics, communications, and education. Siri, the voice activated personal assistant found in the Apple iPhone, was the brain child of SRI. SRI is an idea machine and SRI's CEO, Curtis Carlson, credits its success in producing so many breakthrough innovations to a very systematic approach to idea development and evaluation, called NABC: Needs, Approach, Benefits (per costs), and Competition. An idea must state what customer needs it addresses, how the problem will be solved—the approach, what customer benefits this approach will bring, and what the competitors offer and at what cost. The NABC idea evaluation technique is at the heart of SRI and the entire Silicon Valley Venture Capital community. It is an excellent technique for evaluating new products or services, but it does not meld easily when you are improving existing products. Keeping these core principles in mind, I have developed four questions that are more relevant in the context of sustained innovations and are much easier for employees to understand and answer.

Idea Questions:

1. **Name:** What is the name for the idea?

2. **Description:** What is a brief description of the idea, including what problem it addresses and how it solves it?

3. **Benefits**: What value or benefits will the idea deliver to the customer or company?

4. **Cost-Benefit Rationale:** How much will it cost to try or implement the idea? Does the cost justify the benefits?

This information is like a mini-business case for the idea. For an idea to be accepted and implemented, the employee must provide answers to all of these questions. These questions act as a first line filter that weeds out many of the silly ideas. They push employees to think through their ideas, step outside their comfort zones, interact with subject matter experts from various units, and learn more about the business. This process fosters new kinds of interaction and spurs intelligent dialogue among employees. Suddenly, the technical staff wants to learn about marketing, and the marketing staff is learning about how the technology works. This is perhaps the best business education and cross-training program you can implement without incurring any additional expenses. These questions are the basic fundamentals of any business decision.

Management does cost-benefit analysis all the time. So, instead of you performing the cost-benefit analysis, you are pushing these decisions down and growing your people. Anyone who wants to grow and develop his or her business skills must learn these basic principles.

People sometimes view asking too many questions as a creativity killer—especially, the cost-benefit rationale question. I frequently remind people that this program is not designed to be a brainstorming session. Brainstorming sessions are designed to solicit as many ideas as possible, and then the facilitator goes away to weed through ideas to make sense of them. The goal of the innovation program is not to collect as many ideas as possible. You don't need the overhead of reviewing and evaluating undeveloped ideas and then spending time in explaining why the ideas don't make sense or what additional information is needed for them to become valid ideas. Quality is much more important than quantity. Most of the ideas generated through this program will be improvements to existing products, processes, and systems. Often there are business reasons why management decided to use one approach over the other, and you don't want to be in a situation where you constantly have to explain why you decided to go with the current approach, material, or design.

Without these questions, you will get a flood of ideas that serve personal interests, benefit a handful of customers, or simply don't make sense. For example, let's consider that you are looking for ideas to bring more people to your new grocery store. The recent high school graduate you hired suggests offering a free car wash to shoppers. After all, this was the best idea at his school fundraiser.

Yes, offering a free car wash has high potential for driving traffic, but is it a very practical idea? What is the cost of a car wash in comparison to the average profit per customer per visit? Is it possible to get a permit for a car wash in the commercial park where the store is located, and would other tenants allow it? You think I am exaggerating? Trust me; I have seen worse suggestions, despite asking all those questions. I am intentionally not sharing those examples to make sure I don't defame anyone.

There will be times when an employee cannot produce cost-benefit analyses because he does not know how the market will respond to the solution or change. In those circumstances, you should evaluate the idea based on what value it adds, how you would test the market, and how much time and money it will cost to try it out. In Chapter Nine, we will discuss forming an Idea Steering Committee responsible for evaluating and recommending ideas for implementation. You need to encourage employees to talk to the Idea Steering Committee for help developing business cases for their ideas. Sometimes, the employee submitting the idea has no clue where to find the information, so it's okay to submit an idea without all that information. The Idea Steering Committee can help connect the employee with appropriate domain experts to answer all their questions.

All the information mentioned here is time tested. While producing this information is hard in the beginning, it's an important step for employee education and developing critical thinking skills. To make it easier on employees, especially in the early stages of the program, you might choose to forgo asking all the questions. But as the program catches on, you will have many ideas flowing in until the Idea Steering Committee becomes the bottleneck. Therefore, at some point, you will have to reenact these rules and push the first level of idea evaluation down to the employee submitting the idea. The cost-benefit rationale, or return on investment (ROI) analysis, will also help prioritize ideas for implementation. You will receive a wide range of ideas, some of which may cost a few hours of someone's time, while others may need to be escalated to the corporate project level. Having the cost-benefit analysis embedded into the idea also lets the employee know how quickly his or her idea will be implemented. Remember, it is *not* a numerical ROI calculation that causes analysis-paralysis; nor should it be an exhaustive business case, but rather, a simple explanation that makes employees think in a more holistic manner.

IDEA-CAPTURING SOFTWARE

Numerous idea-capturing software solutions are already available in the marketplace, and new players are popping up to capitalize on the heightened corporate interest in implementing such programs. The growing number of software solutions catering to this market suggest that such initiatives are no longer an isolated phenomenon. Companies are realizing the power of such programs and actively looking for ways to engage employees in generating new ideas.

At the core, these software solutions are nothing but a simple, web-based form that allows you to fill out a handful of data fields. The data is stored in a central database so you can run reports and metrics to monitor the program's health. Most of these systems are ready for use out of the box, and they offer tremendous flexibility, letting you create your own data fields, change labels, and create custom process flows to meet your needs.

List of features to look for in an Idea-Capturing Tool:

1. **Idea Submission Page:** A simple webpage that lets you enter an idea with title and description. Ideally, the system should allow you to ask basic questions like the name and description first, and subsequently, ask additional questions to develop a business case for the idea. The ability to ask additional questions is particularly helpful if you are breaking down these questions into smaller questions to help employees evaluate their ideas. You can also choose to ask all the business case questions upfront. In essence, the system should be flexible enough to allow you to ask the idea questions in one or multiple pages. Be sure to have helpful descriptions for each question, briefly explaining what the question means. The system should also allow for uploading attachments and adding links to external sources for reference.

2. **Versioning:** The system should allow you to update and revise ideas. Ideas rarely emerge fully formed or stay in their original form, so as ideas are updated with time, it is helpful if the system has a built-in mechanism for retaining old information. In the software world, this feature is called versioning.

3. **Enforce Rules:** The system should give you the control to determine which data fields are required and which are optional. In addition, the system should offer the flexibility to change the data fields, labels, and rules as the program matures, without losing historical data.

4. **Process Flow:** The system needs a built-in process flow that can be used to assign ideas to appropriate leaders. An idea may get assigned to team leads, subject matter experts, or go back to the employee who submitted the idea for more information. The system should also have the ability to assign ideas to different team members as the ideas progress through different stages from discovery to implementation. We will discuss the idea stages in Chapter Nine.

5. **Discussions and Notifications:** This feature is very effective for starting a dialogue around an idea. A good system should allow you to start a discussion around an idea, submit relevant documents, and send email notifications as the ideas are discussed, updated, or moved through different stages. Employees should be able to subscribe to the newsfeed of ideas, so they can follow the ideas that interest them.

6. **Reports and Dashboards:** No system is complete without reporting. The Idea-Capturing System is no exception. The system should have built in reports to mine the data, but more importantly, it needs a dashboard that displays the total number of ideas submitted, number of ideas accepted, number of ideas implemented, and activities around ideas. This is a very important feature to help you manage the process, engage employees, and showcase progress. This dashboard should be the centerpiece of your company intranet.

Many tools are out there in the market, so I am intentionally not listing names to avoid endorsement. Many of these tools offer additional features like Mobile App, Keyword Tagging, Related Ideas, Team Formation, and other project life cycle management features. These are all helpful features, but they are not critical. If you are budget constrained and feel that you cannot afford a new system, you still have options. You can take any open-source discussion software and customize the fields or use an existing system that can be customized to capture this information. When I started this program, I was aggressively cutting cost and had no extra money to spend to buy another system. Additionally, I didn't even know whether what I was doing was going to be successful; nor did I know what to look for in all of this information. The whole concept started from my employee engagement experiments and morphed into an idea generation tool. I used our existing intranet technology and created a simple web-form to capture ideas. It did not take too much time to create a simple website that did the job.

The Idea-Capturing System does not have to be complex. All you need is a simple web-page with a handful of data input fields. That said, having a well-designed Idea-Capturing System can aid the adoption process, and you can focus your energy on promoting the program rather than dealing with software bugs, which end up discouraging employees from submitting ideas. Implementing an Idea-Capturing System alone is not enough to encourage employees to submit ideas. In the next chapter, I'll discuss how to encourage and support employees in developing and submitting ideas.

RECAP

- Employees get the best ideas while doing their daily job—so an easily accessible system increases the likelihood that they will submit ideas.

- The existence of such a system/tool entices people to think up and submit ideas.

- Asking the right questions is critical to getting good ideas. These questions should guide employees in how to build a business case for their ideas.

- Many software solutions are already available to capture ideas. The software of choice should be configurable, flexible, and easy to use.

- Good dashboards and reports are essential to measuring the program's success and enticing employees to submit more ideas.

Chapter Seven Exercises

Q1. What core features and functions do you want in your Idea-Capturing System?

_____

_____

_____

_____

_____

_____

_____

_____

_____

Q2. Who will be accessing the Idea-Capturing System, and what functions will they be performing? For example: Employees—Submitting/Updating Idea; Idea Steering Committee—Administration, Reporting and Task Assignments; Senior Management—Dashboards etc.

_____

_____

_____

_____

Q3. What will the idea process flow look like from the employee's perspective?

_____

_____

_____

_____

_____

_____

Q4. Is it a self-managed system or hosted Cloud solution? Is it accessible to all the participants whom you want to enroll in submitting ideas?

_____

_____

_____

_____

Q5. What questions do you want an idea submitter to answer when submitting an idea?

_____

_____

_____

_____

_____

Q6. How do you plan to conduct your search for vendors and solutions, and evaluate various solutions?

_____

_____

_____

_____

_____

_____

Chapter 8

Step 3: Support
Assuring Commitment

The difference between "involvement" and "commitment"
is like an eggs-and-ham breakfast: the chicken was
"involved"—the pig was "committed."
— Anonymous

Every initiative requires some investment, whether it is time, resources, or money. Implementing a bottom-up innovation program is no exception. It is a cultural transformation initiative, but thankfully, unlike many other culture change initiatives, implementing a bottom-up innovation program does not require a complete corporate shakeup or a lot of upfront capital investment. The most important thing employees need is support and encouragement from management, and a little bit of freedom to contemplate and develop ideas.

Creating an environment where management encourages employees to submit and develop ideas is the most important investment you need to make. You need to create an environment where employees feel comfortable bringing out the issues inside the company, flaws in the business processes, and weaknesses in your products. Employees will not submit any good ideas until they are confident there will be no negative repercussions for pointing out organizational weaknesses. You have to earn employees' trust. The actions of each and every manager, supervisor, and executive must reflect that it is okay to challenge norms and existing processes. Management must want employee input and ideas. You need to assure employees through your actions that you are interested in hearing those ideas. By implementing this program, you have already taken strides in earning their trust, but you also need to train all managers to say, "Do I hear an idea?" or "That sounds like a great idea" or "How about we develop this concept and submit it as an idea?" They can also hand down one of their ideas to one of their team members to encourage participation.

Top management commitment has to be more than just an agreement to implement this program. Management must show commitment through everyday actions and decisions. Using Toyota again as an example, when Toyota launched its initiative, it listed "Quality Improvement" as its top priority. Toyota was so committed to this goal that it empowered its front-line workers to stop the assembly line if quality standards were not met. Any worker, regardless of his rank and responsibilities, could pull a cord strung along the assembly line to call for assistance if he detected a defect or production set-up problem that could compromise quality. When the cord was pulled, the "andon" display board would light up and the team leader would come to help. The assembly line is resumed only after the problem is fixed or mediated, ensuring that the part is assembled correctly. Only then is the vehicle sent to the next process. If the problem cannot be fixed in time, the assembly line is stopped and the car is not sent on to the next process until it is fixed. Detroit automakers, on the other hand, were very interested in improving quality, but would have never tolerated a front-line employee stopping the entire production line. This is the difference between commitment and agreement.

Let's discuss the more tangible investment you need to make to support the program. There are four major points of investment:

1. Idea-Capturing System

2. Employee Time

3. Seed Capital

4. Implementation Resources

As we discussed in the previous chapter, you need an Idea-Capturing System to capture employee ideas. I would recommend that you do your due diligence and buy a good system with all the bells and whistles that creates an emotional appeal for employees and lets them participate in any way or shape they want. Your goal should be to make it easy for employees to access and use the system. Employees should be able to access the system from their mobile phones, tablets, or anywhere with Internet access. You never know when they might stumble across an ingenious idea. The best ideas often come to us when we are in a totally different environment and not performing our day-to-day tasks. I know I get my best ideas in the shower or when I am on vacation. These systems are relatively inexpensive and available in both pay-per-use

Cloud models and in-house installations. At the core, these systems are simply a web-form to capture some basic information and a handful of add-on features.

Another important investment you need to make is employee time. You need to decide on how much time you are willing to give employees to experiment with or develop ideas. Employees need time to contemplate, write ideas down, and network with peers to brainstorm ideas. 3M led the revolution of employee innovation by allowing employees to use 15 percent of their time to work on their pet projects. Google took it to the next level by setting aside 20 percent of employees' time to work on new ideas. W.L. Gore sets aside 10 percent of an employee's time to experiment and try new ideas. Setting aside dedicated time for experimentation will give a good boost to the program, but it is not absolutely necessary in the early stages of program development. If you don't already have a culture of experimentation embedded in your company culture, the dedicated experimentation time will turn into idle time and do more harm than good. That said, employees do need some time to develop ideas, collect additional data, and work with subject matter experts to build a business case for their ideas. This exercise does not require a lot of time, and managers should encourage those who have ideas to spend time developing them. Once the program has developed roots in the organization, you can start allotting explicit experimentation time.

Do not equate the dedicated experimentation time to lost productivity. Allotting 10 percent experimentation time does not mean that you are suddenly cutting your employee productivity by 10 percent. Your employees already waste this time and much more in idle chit-chat, coffee breaks, and web-surfing. Social interaction adds a lot of value to building relationships, learning, collaboration, and cross-training, but if they are only discussing last night's TV shows, they are not adding value to anyone. In contrast, when you implement this program, you turn employees into idea hunters. Then, their subconscious minds are always looking for ideas, and these social interactions morph into more intelligent idea discussions. Many organizations report that employee productivity went up after implementing such an initiative. Most companies, including Google, Apple, and PIXAR, have built designated spaces for employees to engage in idea exchange dialogue.

Lastly, money is an important element when thinking of implementing such a program. You need to decide how you are going to fund the ideas and projects that will emerge from this process. The most common practice is to set aside some seed money to back experiments and fund various small ideas. Ideally, the innovation program should have its own budget for operations, funding small isolated projects, and celebrating and rewarding employees for implemented ideas. But be careful; do not instill a culture that limits spending because the budget has run out or that believes we must spend the budgeted money in this fiscal year. This practice is prevalent in many organizations, which is the byproduct of our age-old financial management practices. Do your best to avoid creating this type of mindset. As part of the innovation program budget, allocate a pool of funds—more as a guideline than a hard line—for idea implementation. And management has to be comfortable with this concept. Ideas should compete for funding and resources based on merit, and no idea should be funded without a valid business case. All ideas worth pursuing will present valid business cases and justify their funding needs. For governance, you can give the Idea Steering Committee the authority to approve ideas up to a certain dollar amount, and all ideas beyond this threshold will be referred to management for approval. All companies need to account for operational spending for forecasting, planning, and expense management purposes, but some companies like to have tight control over budgeted versus non-budgeted spending, so you need to make decisions ensuring you have enough money and resources available to implement all valid ideas.

In addition to setting up a budget for the innovation program, you will also need to make room in the corporate and departmental resources to implement new projects emerging out of this process. Even companies that set aside dedicated time for employees to work on their ideas have to make room in corporate resources to push the promising ideas to the next level. For most companies, the employee submitting the idea may not have the necessary skills to implement or try the idea. The idea must be passed on to subject matter experts or the appropriate departments for implementation. In my own experience, and others I have talked to have said the same: most of the early ideas tend to be technology-related. In my case, since I manage the Information Technology (IT) department and I created the innovation program, I had a vested interest in supporting the program and finding room in the budget to implement these ideas. But your innovation leader may not have direct influence over IT; you need to make sure you have strong buy-in from IT since it will be taking on ad hoc projects emerging out of this effort. We will discuss this topic in-depth in Chapter Ten when we discuss execution, but for now, you need to keep in mind that you will need resources from the entire organization to implement ideas.

Managers at every level must encourage and support employees in thinking of new ways things can be done more effectively or differently that will add value for the customer, company, and all the stakeholders. However, once you have all the systems and processes in place and open the gate to all employees, you will get all sorts of ideas. You need some means to sort through the noise and prioritize good ideas for implementation. In the next chapter, we will discuss how to create a central body responsible for validating, refining, and prioritizing ideas.

RECAP

- All managers should encourage employees to participate in the program and come up with ideas that help the business.
- Four types of investments are needed for a bottom-up innovation program: Idea-Capturing System, Employee Time, Seed Money, and Implementation Resources.
- Set-aside some money to fund ongoing and small ideas.
- Create an environment where it is okay for employees to challenge conventions, processes, and decisions.
- Support employees and help them carve out some time to develop their ideas.

Chapter Eight Exercises

Q1. What intangible means do you plan to use to support and encourage employees to think of ideas that will improve the business?

_____

_____

_____

_____

_____

_____

Q2. What capital and resource investments will you need to support the program? Write an estimated dollar value for each item.

_____

_____

_____

_____

_____

_____

Chapter 9

Step 4: Triage Screening Ideas

All that glitters is not gold.
— William Shakespeare

The next step in building the bottom-up employee innovation program is to create effective means for screening and prioritizing ideas. Despite good intentions, employees will not always be submitting ideas that are aligned with your organizational goals or vetted to make sure they make business sense. Especially in the program's early days, there will be plenty of ideas—from installing "compost bins" to initiating "beer Thursdays"—that do not belong in the Bright Idea Box. You need some means and guidelines to review, approve, or reject ideas. The best way to accomplish this is to form an Idea Screening Committee that meets on a regular basis to review newly submitted ideas and discuss changes to existing ideas.

The name Idea Steering Committee clearly communicates this group's purpose and authority, but the name did not sit well with my team. Before rolling out the program to the entire company, I ran it by my team members to get their input and perspectives. After all, they had been a big part of this experiment. The strongest objection I got was on the use of the name "Idea Steering Committee." Luckily, I am blessed with a team that is full of ideas, and they suggested calling this group the "Idea Support Team." This name change proved invaluable in earning employee trust and building a strong working relationship between employees and the Idea Support Team. Group activities suddenly became more of a peer review process than just a filter for ideas. You can also play with the name as you see fit. I also have seen organizations call it the "Innovation Council." Ideally, the name should convey the sense that this is a peer support group—a committee comprised of fellow employees whose job is to help employees strengthen their ideas, develop a business case, and see their ideas through to completion.

IDEA SUPPORT TEAM (IST):

The Idea Support Team (IST) should be made up of three or four line level employees, plus the innovation leader.

It is best if the Idea Support Team is mostly comprised of non-management members. These employees will play a vital role in promoting the program and encouraging fellow employees to submit ideas. When employees are contemplating new ideas, they will need help articulating and developing a business case for their ideas. Employees will find it much easier to talk to peers rather than members of management when fleshing out their ideas. I also noticed that employees gave each other very candid feedback when an idea did not have a good business case. The dialogue tends to be much more open and educational than when a manager delivers the same message.

IST is also a liaison between employees, management, subject matter experts, and the implementation teams. It is IST's job to review every idea and determine whether it has a valid business case. Another important function of IST is to make sure that ideas stay true to the mission of the innovation program. All ideas should add value for customers and support business objectives outlined in the purpose document. If the idea does not contribute to business goals, it does not belong in the Bright Idea Box. When the idea costs more than the value it delivers, or when there is not an effective way to implement it, then it needs to be flagged for further refinement.

IST should meet on a regular basis, ideally once a week, or every other week, depending on the volume of ideas, to review the newly submitted ideas and discuss any new development on existing ideas. IST reviews the changes and tracks progress through different stages of the idea life cycle.

The idea life cycle and its progress can be tracked through the following five stages:

1. New Submission

2. Under Review

3. Needs Development

4. Accepted

5. Implemented

When a new idea is submitted, it will be at the "New Submission" stage. After IST reviews the idea, it may decide that the team needs input from subject matter experts or needs further clarification from the employee who submitted the idea. Also, there will be times when an idea has potential, but the employee does not have the capacity to develop a good business case for the idea. Under these circumstances, IST may decide to solicit opinions from subject matter experts and move the idea to the "Under Review" stage. If the idea has no apparent business value or business case, it is moved to the "Needs Development" stage. At this stage, it is up to the employee who submitted the idea to refine the idea and work with IST to develop a good business case. All ideas in the "Needs Development" stage are up for grabs. Someone else may have a better way to achieve the idea's underlying goal or may suggest implementing the same concept in a more cost-effective way. He or she can choose to collaborate with the originator or completely take over the idea. Ideas with a valid business case move to the "Accepted" stage, and once the ideas are implemented, they move to the final "Implemented" stage. IST is responsible for pushing ideas for implementation. IST should be actively reviewing and updating the progress of ideas until they are implemented.

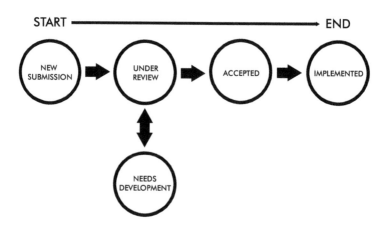

Idea Process Flow and Stages

You also need to develop communication protocols and expectations for IST. The long-term success of the program depends on how well IST communicates progress with different stakeholders. Employees who submit ideas need quick and timely feedback to let them know the results of IST's initial evaluation. If the idea is accepted, quick notification will boost morale, and if the idea needs further development, the employee can decide how he or she would like to proceed. Often, employees will be quick to submit ideas without thinking through the effect on the business, and most of them will drop the idea when someone asks them for more information on how the idea adds value or what business challenges it solves. But you have given them the choice. If they feel strongly about the ideas and are passionate about them, they can work with IST and subject matter experts to develop their ideas further.

To ensure that employees are not discouraged when their ideas are not accepted, IST must practice a fair and transparent process for evaluating ideas based on the guidelines outlined in the purpose statement. The purpose statement will be a tremendous help for IST members when they have to reject ideas. Then they don't have to be the bad guys because they can build the rationale for rejecting the idea based on the program guidelines rather than themselves.

Here's a sample charter for IST that can serve as a guide as well as a means to hold it accountable for following fair practices and standards.

IST CHARTER:

- Meet on regular basis to review ideas.
- Make sure the ideas and the program stay true to the program's mission.
- Encourage fellow employees to submit ideas.
- Recognize employees for their contributions.
- Communicate with idea submitters in a timely manner and keep them informed during different stages of the idea.
- Act as a liaison between the employees who submit ideas, subject matter experts, and management.
- Assist fellow employees in developing ideas and business cases.
- Develop a fair and transparent process to assess the idea's business value.
- Escalate big and risky ideas to senior management for input and approval.
- Push for implementation of accepted ideas and seek additional funding as needed to implement ideas.

As the program takes hold in the organization, a lot of new ideas will need to be reviewed and old ideas will need to be tracked. IST will need some agreed upon framework to manage this workload. IST can decide to assign specific tasks to its various members, depending on each person's expertise, or divide ideas equally among its members to take complete responsibility for seeing the assigned ideas through to implementation. I recommend the latter because it will serve as a training ground for IST members to develop their leadership and communication skills.

The next logical question is how to select the IST members. During the program rollout phase, you can solicit interest from employees who would like to be part of the Idea Support Team.

Compile the list of interested employees and ask management to vote for their top picks. You can use any technique that you find fits, as long you make sure you have enough diversity in the group. By diversity, I mean members from different parts of the organization with varying degrees of experience and exposure. IST also needs a management member who is the program's executive sponsor and champion. You can put a one-year term limit in place for each of the IST members. Rotation of IST members will help bring fresh perspectives to the program, encourage fair practices, and promote awareness throughout the organization.

Once you have established this screening and support team, you need to empower this team to push the appropriate business units to execute the ideas. In the next chapter, we will discuss how to develop an overarching approach for implementing ideas based on the nature of your business and organizational skill set.

RECAP

- Establish a committee dedicated to screening ideas and promoting the program.
- The Idea Support Team (IST) should be made up of non-management employees and the innovation leader. Most employees find it easier to ask for help from fellow employees than management.
- IST should have a clear charter that defines its role as well as guidelines for screening and recommending ideas for implementation.
- IST must communicate with idea submitters in a timely manner and make constructive recommendations to improve ideas.
- IST must exercise a fair and transparent process.

Chapter Nine Exercises

Q1. How will you screen, prioritize, and recommend ideas for implementation?

_____

_____

_____

_____

_____

_____

_____

Q2. What idea stages would you like to use for tracking idea progress?

_____

_____

_____

_____

_____

_____

_____

Q3. Do you need an Idea Screening Committee (or Idea Support Team/Innovation Council)? If so, what experience, background, and skills must its members have? What is the general make up of this team?

_____

_____

_____

_____

_____

_____

Q4. What will the charter be for your Idea Screening Committee? You can use the charter listed in this chapter and add/remove responsibilities as you see fit.

_____

_____

_____

_____

_____

_____

_____

_____

_____

_____

Chapter 10

Step 5: Execute
Implementing Ideas

An idea is worthless unless you use it.
— John Maxwell

Once an idea has been approved and financed, it must be implemented in a timely manner. Without a clearly visible process and a push from the top, an idea can easily vanish into the vast depths of corporate bureaucracy. As part of designing the program, you need to decide how you are going to test and implement ideas. You need to flush out who is responsible for implementing the ideas and what type of commitment you need from the impacted parties. When applicable, who is responsible for building the prototypes and testing the markets? What resources and commitments can you offer to those involved in implementing the ideas? Everyone in your organization is busy, or at least, each individual thinks he is. Everyone is running lean and has no extra time to take on side projects. If you do not resolve this issue upfront, you will run into serious problems down the road. The queue of "accepted" ideas will keep getting longer, and the employees who submitted the ideas will start getting frustrated with management and losing faith in the program. The program will be viewed as management's lip service to employee empowerment, which will hurt the morale of engaged employees. There is no faster way to kill the innovation program than by not implementing good ideas.

Implementing ideas is where the rubber meets the road. The implementation is an informal type of feedback that shows employees that you value their ideas. The more ideas you implement, the more you will encourage your employees to submit new ideas. There is a high likelihood that some of the projects emerging out of this process will conflict for resources with existing projects, so it is very important that you think through how these projects will fit into your existing portfolio of projects and corporate priorities. Every idea, from small to large, will require resources, time, and in some cases, additional funding, so you need to make sure that the organization is ready to make room for these additional projects. Most of the projects emerging from the Bright Idea Box will be small, and they may not carry enough weight to compete for resources against the corporate projects. Therefore, you will have to elevate the program to be a corporate priority and make sure everyone in management is onboard, especially internal service departments like Information Technology, Corporate Resources Management, and the Program Management Office, which may all be involved in implementing these projects.

The next logical question is: Are there any best practices for implementing ideas? Do you give employees time off from their regular jobs to work on special projects, increase the budget and resources across all departments, or hire dedicated teams to work on special projects? Unfortunately, there is no single straightforward answer. Your implementation approach will depend on the culture of your organization, the skill-set of your employees, and the nature of the ideas you anticipate.

As stated earlier, Google gives its employees 20 percent of their working hours to work on side projects that emerge from employee ideas. This approach works well for Google, since large numbers of its employees are computer engineers. Google is in the information management business and encourages employees to develop ideas around information management. Most of the employees have the basic programming skills to develop prototypes for their ideas. Once an employee has developed the concept, it can be used to recruit more team members and seek funding and permission to test the market. Depending on the market response, Google's management can decide whether the idea deserves more funding or it needs a more seasoned product manager to grow the idea. This approach has been very effective for Google, and some of its best and most profitable products have come out of this 20 percent time. Google News is one example of such personal-time projects. After the September 11, 2001 attacks on the Twin Towers, Krishna Bharat, a Google employee, felt the need to aggregate news from different news sites to keep him abreast of what was being discussed around the world, especially his home country of India. He created an aggregator program that fetched news from various credible news sites and brought them to one place based on his preferences. He realized that others could also benefit from a news aggregator so he showcased his idea to management. He got the funding to create the Google News website, which delivers news to users based on their preferences. Google News gained popularity so quickly that its success convinced Google management to bring Google News into one of its strategic portfolios of services. At that point, Google management assigned a more experienced product manager, Marissa Mayer, to take Google News to the next level. Today, Google News is the primary source of news for billions of people across the globe.

If the nature of your business is such that most of your employees are well-versed in the basic skills needed to create new products—for example, a software company where most of the employees know how to write code and can easily produce the end product or the prototype—then setting aside dedicated experimentation time for employees to work on new ideas makes the most sense. Let the person who came up with the idea also create the product and you can test the product by offering it to a limited market. You can develop guidelines based around capital investment, how to test the market, and when to put more resources or a more experienced team in place to develop the product further. This approach works best for high-tech companies and companies with established R&D culture and staff. 3M was the first company to develop this technique of offering a product to a limited market. 3M had a diverse workforce, but it also had a strong R&D culture and employees had access to resources that could help them with design and prototypes.

Many new start-up companies are embedding such practices into their culture and expecting employees to spend time working on new ideas. If setting aside time feels like a bit of a stretch and you don't think you will be able to convince management or mobilize your workforce, start with an annual or quarterly innovation contest where employees either work toward a specific challenge or develop a feature or product in one day. These contests are often referred as Hackathons. With time, you can refine the program and shorten the gap between these idea contests based on what worked and what didn't. Personally, I always give everyone time to get acclimated to a new thinking process before embedding dedicated experimentation time into everyone's job description.

Most businesses, however, are not like Google and 3M, so this approach is not very practical for most of them. In a typical business setting, the employee who came up with the idea doesn't necessarily have the skill or access to the resources to develop and test the ideas. For example, a customer service employee notices that a lot of customers are calling to reset their passwords, even though the website offers the feature to let customers reset their own passwords. After talking to the customers, she concludes that the customers are calling out of frustration because the forgotten password link on the website is not very intuitive. Her idea is to make the "Forgotten Password" feature available on the same screen that displays the login failure message. It should lessen the customers' frustration and reduce the number of incoming calls, which will add value to both the customers and the company. She knows what she wants to try out, but she doesn't know how to do it. She has no knowledge of how the website works and no programming skills to test her idea. She needs help from the technology department or the webmaster. In this scenario, it is best for the Idea Support Team to channel the idea to the appropriate department, in this case the IT department, for testing and implementing the idea.

Passing ideas to experts for implementation is perhaps the most obvious approach for businesses with a diverse workforce or businesses that cannot afford to allot dedicated experimentation time. This approach sounds simple, but it is not as straightforward as it sounds. The first challenge is to make sure that the experts or the affected business units have room to take on these projects. Most companies like to plan for projects and allocate resources in their annual planning processes, and they decide upfront which projects to take on in any given year based on human and capital resources. This approach cannot work for this program since you don't know which and how many ideas you will be getting in a year. It is hard to plan resources and capital upfront. The only reasonable solution to this problem is to allocate some resources upfront and then be open to change. Top management has to be comfortable with not planning for 100 percent utilization of the resources and with trusting the line managers to use resources effectively. Not planning for 100 percent utilization is almost like giving 10-20 percent time to work on side projects, but in this case, you may have to allocate 30 or 40 percent of time to the most affected units like Information Technology and make some room in other business units since an idea can involve any department. In other words, the entire company has to be prepared to work on any ad hoc projects emerging out this process, but some departments, like IT, will be more affected than others. That is where you will need to make the most room. Support departments like IT must also welcome these projects and build a strong culture of collaboration with idea originators. The biggest challenge is that the ideas never emerge fully formed in their final state. Implementation teams have to work collaboratively with the idea originator and IST. Sometimes, the subject matter expert may have a better way of solving the same challenge, and at other times, the implementation process uncovers new challenges that push the cost up until, suddenly, cost outweighs the benefits. It is then up to IST to decide which path to take and inform all the parties involved in the idea implementation.

Regardless of the approach, the involvement of the idea originator is critical in all phases of the idea life cycle. The idea submitter must champion her idea. She cannot submit an idea and walk away from it. She has to push for her idea to be implemented and must work closely with subject matter experts and implementation teams. Nobody is likely to be more passionate about having the idea implemented than the one who submitted it. At the end of the process, there is a prize and recognition for each implemented idea. Idea generators have to work on their ideas to earn that recognition. You will find many ideas lingering in the "Needs Development" stage. Often employees will submit the idea, but then they will not work on developing the business case or collecting additional data to prove its validity. IST should not be responsible for chasing idea submitters, but rather, idea submitters have to stay engaged and seek help from IST and subject matter experts to bring their ideas to life.

Just by the nature of the program, employees will be submitting all sorts of ideas, from minor tweaks in the business process to ones that challenge the business' strategic direction. The implementation approach will vary widely depending on the nature of the idea, but the Idea Support Team can be the central command post for disseminating ideas to appropriate departments. All ideas are reviewed and refined by IST for their validity. When needed,

IST seeks help from management to prioritize ideas and pass them on to the appropriate implementation teams, subject matter experts, or business units for implementation. The diagram below illustrates the flow of idea implementation:

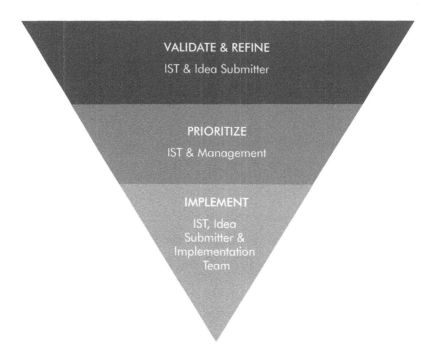

To make this process work, IST needs support from top management and access to all department managers. From time to time, IST may need help from management in prioritizing projects or getting additional resources for implementation. It is helpful if a member of senior management sponsors the program, sits in the IST group meetings, and pushes various groups to implement ideas. This sponsorship will also reduce the need to seek approval for every little project. One of the Idea Support Team's responsibilities should be to determine who should be involved in each stage, including senior management. IST can decide to pass the idea to the appropriate department, involve subject matter experts, management, or lead the project in its entirety. Ultimately, IST is responsible for accepting, rejecting, and prioritizing ideas based on the business case and value.

Once an idea is implemented, you need to recognize the employee for submitting a good idea and all the effort that he or she put into building a valid business case and working with various groups to implement it. In the next chapter, we will discuss various intrinsic and extrinsic means for recognizing employees.

RECAP

- There is no one implementation approach that works across all industries or ideas.

- If the majority of your employees have the same basic skills, give employees dedicated experimentation time to test and implement ideas.

- If your workforce is diverse, use IST to delegate ideas to appropriate business units for implementation.

- Delegate some authority to the IST to eliminate the need to go to management for every little idea.

- Get all department heads on board so new ideas will be adopted by business units and to make sure the resources are available to implement the idea.

- Idea submitters must champion their ideas and be involved and available throughout the idea's life cycle.

Chapter Ten Exercises

Q1. What implementation strategy will work best in your environment?

_____

_____

_____

Q2. What will the idea progress flow look like, from new submission to implementation, under this strategy?

_____

_____

_____

_____

_____

_____

Q3. What additional funding and implementation resources will you need to implement ideas emerging out of this process?

_____

_____

_____

_____

_____

_____

Q4. Which business units will be most affected by the ad hoc work created by this initiative? List all the business units from which you will need support to take on the additional work created by this program.

_____

_____

_____

_____

_____

_____

Q5. What role does the Idea Support Committee play in the implementation process?

_____

_____

_____

Chapter 11

Step 6: Recognize Recognizing Employees

Appreciation is a wonderful thing: It makes what is excellent in others belong to us as well.
— Voltaire

The final step in developing the program is deciding how to recognize employees for their ideas and efforts. Recognition is the lifeline of the Bright Idea Box. Setting the right kinds of rewards is critical to the program's longevity and ensuring that employees stay motivated to submit new ideas. Recognition is an opportunity to encourage desired behaviors and reward employees for thinking and acting in ways that add value for customers and the company.

Developing a good rewards system is not an easy feat. No two people are motivated by the same thing, and no two ideas carry the same value. In addition, just because a recognition and rewards system worked for one company does not guarantee that it will work for another company. Yet rewards have to be meaningful, fair, and easy to administer. The most important component of any reward has to be its meaning and value to the recipient. Recognition has to have both tangible and intangible elements, and the emphasis on one over the other will depend heavily on the socioeconomic standing of the employees working inside the company.

Maslow's Hierarchy of Needs is a good tool for understanding what motivates and engages people and for assessing the needs of your employees. You can then use this information to develop a reward system that will meet the needs of most employees. The tool is derived from Abraham Maslow, a great twentieth century American psychologist, who published an iconic paper in 1943 that described a hierarchical chart of basic human needs and how those needs shape human behavior on a macro level. This publication has been regarded as a hallmark in the field of psychology, and the chart later became known as Maslow's Hierarchy of Needs.

MASLOW'S HIERARCHY OF NEEDS:

1. Physiological—Food, Water, Shelter, Sleep

2. Safety—Security, Order, Stability

3. Social—Friendship, Family, Intimacy

4. Esteem—Self-Esteem, Confidence, Achievement, Respect of others and by others

5. Self-Actualization—Meaning, Acceptance of Facts, Morality, Lack of Prejudice

MASLOW'S HIERARCHY OF NEEDS

Maslow suggested that our macro-level behavior is driven by which of our needs are already met and which needs we are trying to fulfill. These needs are very hierarchical in nature. Once our basic physiological needs like food, water, sleep, and shelter are adequately met, we shift our focus to safeguarding our self, our loved ones, our belongings, and our surplus. Humans have always sought safety in numbers, which has turned us into very social beings. We yearn for belonging, friendship, family, and intimacy. We first seek social acceptance, and then we move on to establishing our individual identity and self-esteem. We work hard to achieve goals, earn respect from others, and build confidence in our abilities. Lastly, when all of the first four needs are met, we start to look for a deeper meaning and purpose in our existence. Life is very dynamic, so we are constantly going back and forth, trying to satisfy these needs as our life circumstances change, and our actions and behaviors are motivated by the needs we are trying to fulfill. However, the changes in these needs are not everyday occurrences, so you can make general assumptions about the people inside your organization and what kinds of rewards will best meet their needs.

You can review the socioeconomic standing of most of your employees and use Maslow's Hierarchy of Needs to determine which rewards will best motivate them. For example, if you are running a mining company in a Third World country, chances are that your employees are struggling to fulfill their physiological needs. Contrarily, if you are managing a volunteer-run humanitarian organization, your volunteers might be motivated by reassurance of self-actualization. I suspect that most readers of this book will find their employees trying to fulfill their self-esteem needs. Most of us are driven by achievements, respect, recognition, and identity. People do wonderful, as well as stupid, things to fulfill this need. Money plays an important role, since many of our needs can be temporarily fulfilled using things we can buy. However, studies have shown that money starts to become less of a motivator after a certain income threshold, and money does not last long.

LEVELS OF RECOGNITION

Ideally, employees should be recognized for every effort they put toward thinking up and submitting ideas. But in the program's initial months, employees will be submitting ideas that are more self-centered rather than ideas that benefit the company or the customer. To get around this problem, I recommend recognizing employees at only two levels:

- Accepted ideas
- Implemented ideas

Once an idea is accepted, the employee should be recognized for submitting a good idea. I recommend recognizing employees when an idea is accepted and again when the idea is implemented. Recognizing employees for an accepted idea is important since there will be times when the idea is valid but management decides to postpone implementing the idea for various business reasons, including the idea not being a high priority, not being cohesive with other activities, or simply for lack of resources. Nevertheless, the idea is valid; it should be accepted and the employee should be recognized for submitting a valid idea.

It is always nice to get a little extra money for the extra effort you put in at work. Money is a tangible thing, and it can be a good motivator to get people to do something new. But extrinsic rewards, like monetary compensation, have an inherent flaw. Extrinsic rewards tend to lose value with time and often fail to motivate many. Research shows that money does a good job of motivating someone to do something in the beginning, but it does not maintain its appeal or encourage continuous behavior. Giving ten dollars to your teenager will motivate her to take the trash out once or twice, but soon she will need twenty to do the same work.

Monetary compensation could also backfire in some instances. If an idea takes off and the company is now making millions, the employee will hold a grudge if he or she only received a few hundred dollars, while company executives are cashing in. There are also well-documented cases where an employee sued the company for not properly compensating him for his contribution. It is natural for employees to measure the worth of their ideas in proportion to the revenue generated by those ideas—even though it took huge amounts of corporate resources, time, and millions in marketing to bring that idea to fruition. Employees are not always able to see the effort that went into bringing their ideas to life. Even Google suffered from a monetary compensation system. Google created a "Founders' Awards" program in which it gave stock options to employees for implemented ideas, but the program soon backfired. With stock grant prices as low as thirty cents in 2002, the steep rise in Google stock made many millionaires while leaving others very sore about their timings and the projects they worked on. In 2007, Google decided to end its Founders' Awards program and replace it with more intangible things like a thank you visit and the opportunity to discuss ideas with company founders Larry Page and Sergey Brin.

To create a lasting effect, it is best if the recognition is given in the form of intrinsic rewards, with moderate extrinsic rewards. Good examples of intrinsic rewards can be: the innovators of the month, a recognition pin or memento, paid time off, or a party to recognize employees for their contributions. Submitting ideas is a voluntary activity, and to encourage participation, you need to call on employees' higher drive and offer an opportunity to make a difference. Imagine this situation: You are moving and you can use some help from one of your friends. One of these friends happened to have a pick-up truck. What will be more effective in getting that friend to help you: pizza or a twenty dollar bill? The book *100 Ways to Motivate Others* by Steve Chandler is an excellent source of ideas for intrinsic rewards. Intrinsic rewards tend to be slow to take off, and they often stand in comparison to something or someone. That's where the small monetary compensation can help jumpstart the idea flow. A good thing is that you probably have employees in your company who will be ready to submit ideas whether or not they get recognition. You can showcase and celebrate their ideas to motivate others.

You can create a tiered structure, meaning a smaller reward for accepted ideas and a substantially larger reward for implemented ideas. The lure of larger recognition will also motivate employees to champion their ideas toward implementation, and at the same time, to look for ideas that can be quickly implemented and can add immediate value to the company. You can get creative with forms of rewards and give out things that have monetary as well as social value. Examples of such rewards can range from tickets to theme parks or events to fully paid-for family vacation packages. Not only is the employee then happy to receive recognition, but he will be sharing the reward with the loved ones who support and encourage him to work hard at your company. This reward will reinforce employee engagement from multiple directions. Since the reward also has a monetary value, the employee can relate to it both emotionally and monetarily, which creates a much more lasting effect.

We started out by giving a "Bright Idea Pin" for accepted ideas and put the idea generator's picture on the "Wall of Innovators" for implemented ideas. If an employee can display his or her award at work, it motivates other employees to submit ideas. We tack the idea pins outside the employee's cubicle, right next to his or her name tag, where every passerby can see it. The pins serve as conversation starters and are the envy of those who have not submitted any ideas yet. As the employee submits more ideas, he gets more pins to tack outside his cubicle. These pins are symbols of pride.

A growing collection encourages employees to submit more ideas and also creates a healthy competition. For implemented ideas, we took the innovator's picture and put it on a tack board that served as the "Wall of Innovators." Ideally, this board should be placed in a high traffic area where all employees can see it. Every time a new idea gets implemented from the same employee, you can stick a number on the corner, reflecting how many of the employee's ideas were implemented. This process could also serve as a dashboard for the innovation program. You can display how many ideas have been submitted, accepted, and implemented so far. These examples show how you can craft your own recognition system depending on your budget. It can be as simple as a thank you note or as extravagant as Google's Founders' Awards.

I also recommend adding some gamification element to the rewards. You can use virtual currency or points to track progress. For example, every accepted idea gets 100 points, and an implemented idea gets an additional 400 points. At the end of the year, the top ten contributors get a grand prize or employees can redeem these points for other goodies. The points can be displayed on the company intranet or the "Wall of Innovators," where employees can see who is winning and how many ideas they need to reach the Top Ten list. Use your creativity to add as many elements of recognition as you can. Also, nothing is set in stone. If something does not work in your environment, just change it. Word of caution: Whenever you make changes to the reward system, make sure you communicate the changes to employees repeatedly so no one is disappointed at the end-of-the-year tally. The rules should be easy to understand and the progress should be reflected in near real time.

The most important recognition for every employee is praise from the boss. It is critical that managers at all levels encourage and support employees to participate in the program. In the next section, we will discuss the cultural aspect of creating this program and how to get strong buy-in from all the layers of management.

RECAP

- Establish both extrinsic and intrinsic means to recognize employees.

- Recognize employees at two stages: once when their idea is accepted and again when their idea is implemented.

- Money is a short-term motivator. You need to add symbols of praise and recognition to create a lasting effect.

- Use a memento that employees can showcase at work that everyone can see. This will create a desire in employees to earn it.

- Make it into a game. Create points that employees can earn throughout the year for submitting valid ideas. Employees can exchange points for rewards at the end of the year.

Chapter Eleven Exercises

Q1. How can you thank employees for participating in the program? At what stages of an idea would you recognize employees and how?

_____

_____

_____

_____

_____

_____

_____

Q2. For each recognition element, can you list at least three benefits to the employees?

_____

_____

_____

_____

_____

_____

_____

Q3. How and where would you like to display Bright Idea Box statistics? For example: number of ideas Submitted, Accepted, and Implemented.

_____

_____

_____

_____

_____

_____

Q4. Are you planning to use any gaming elements, where employees can earn points for submitting good ideas? If so, how will employees earn points and where will this information be displayed?

_____

_____

_____

_____

_____

_____

- Part Three -

THE ENGAGEMENT

Chapter 12

Leading the Innovation Charter

*If your actions inspire others to dream more, learn more,
do more and become more, you are a leader.*
— John Quincy Adams

It goes without saying that the need for innovation starts at the top. This book shows the mechanics of the bottom-up innovation program, but the vision and guidance has to come from the top. The program's success largely depends on support from the top and the skills of the organization's leaders. There are hundreds of great books on leadership, so I will not spend time repeating leadership qualities, but rather focus on a few specific leadership lessons that are critical to launching a bottom-up innovation program.

Before embarking on this journey, you have to ask yourself what innovation means to you. Do you think this kind of program can work in your organization? Do you believe in your people? Do you think you can teach your employees to think and act like innovators? Who is going to lead this program? Is that innovation leader passionate about getting the best out of people, and can he or she mobilize resources across the entire organization?

Passion, vision, learning, and empowering others are the four key leadership qualities that set great leaders apart from accidental leaders. Jim Collins' book *Good to Great* cites countless examples of leaders who transformed good companies into great companies. They had a clear vision and passion for a better future, hired the right people, empowered people to carry out the vision, and fostered a culture of continuous learning. Passion is also a key ingredient in creating a culture of innovation. If you are not passionate and don't believe in your people, your people will not believe in the program either. Without passion, people think either you don't care or you are not confident. Neither is good for launching this program. Before bringing anyone else on board, you must become a believer. You must believe that ordinary people can do extraordinary things. Below are the four leadership principles that play a vital role in developing and transforming employees into innovators.

DRIVERS OF HIGHER ENGAGEMENT

1. Ownership: Give people responsibility and ownership.

2. Personal Growth: Grow people on a personal level so they can grow professionally.

3. Solution Mindset: Foster a Solution Mindset that promotes progress.

4. Partnership: Treat employees like partners so they will act like partners.

Ownership—Ownership instills a feeling of pride. Nothing motivates people to do more than pride. People work a lot harder for pride and often go to extremes to prove themselves. How can you take advantage of this human condition? Make employees the boss. Give them responsibility. You will be amazed by how someone's IQ increases when you give him or her responsibility. I have seen countless employees, who were written up for poor performance or bad behavior, transform into star employees when they were put in-charge of something. Everyone, to a certain extent, is hungry for power and control. Make every employee in-charge of something—territory, function, system, project, or outcome within a project—anything that will give him or her a sense of ownership and responsibility.

However, some roles and functions don't lend themselves to putting the person in charge of something. You can overcome this challenge by giving employees as much autonomy as possible in performing their jobs and making decisions that influence the outcome of their jobs. Autonomy is perhaps the greatest factor influencing performance. Researchers at Cornell University concluded that companies with a highly autonomous workplace grow at a rate up to four times faster than other companies and reduce turnover by as much as one-third. Malcolm Gladwell made the case in his book *Outliers: The Story of Success* that three things drive our engagement in any task—Autonomy, Complexity, and the Relationship between effort and reward. We are more motivated when we feel we have control over our actions and we can influence the outcome. Give people freedom and control over their actions. State your goals and let them accomplish these goals whichever way they wish. By doing so, you make them responsible for goals, and employees see the outcome of that responsibility as a direct reflection of their abilities and intelligence. They will work extra hard to show that they are capable and intelligent. Howard Schultz, the founder and CEO of Starbucks, is famous for saying, "If you tell people they have what it takes to succeed, they will work hard to prove you right."

Zappos and Whole Foods are two great examples of companies that empower front-line employees by giving them ownership and autonomy regarding customer relation management and making purchasing decisions. There are no scripts and procedures to answering customer calls or buying inventory. These companies share their mission with employees and train them on best practices, but there are no rules to follow—only guidelines to help employees make good decisions and safeguard the company and employees from activities that can adversely affect either one. If an employee makes a wrong decision, his performance is visible to all team members and he is held accountable by his peers. For both companies, this sense of empowerment has created an environment where employees are highly engaged, provide superior customer service, and make good business decisions. The tangible results of this autonomy are clearly visible in the continuous profitability of both companies year after year.

Personal Growth—Growth is the fuel of the soul. Without growth, even the masters can lose interest. In a typical business sense, growth is often associated with promotions and/or an increase in responsibilities. This narrow view of growth limits the possibilities for growth. You cannot promote everyone all the time, yet growth is essential for engagement. To stay engaged, we have to see progress in everything we do. The moment our efforts stop making progress, we start to lose interest and performance declines. The problem here is not growth, but the measurement of growth. Stanford Psychology Professor Carol Dweck has beautifully described the essence of this issue in her book *Mindset: The New Psychology of Success*. Professor Dweck categorizes people into two broader mindsets: "fixed mindset" and "growth mindset." People with a fixed mindset believe that their abilities and talents are fixed, while those with a growth mindset believe that intelligence and abilities can be increased through practice. People with the fixed mindset view every action and decision as a reflection of their intelligence and look to external means like job titles, awards, and recognition as the proof of their intelligence. The growth mindset, on the other hand, is more concerned with learning and the desire to improve. For the fixed mindset, every failure is another push toward a downward spiral that pushes people into depression, while the growth mindset views failure as a signal to work harder. Dr. Dweck argues that the growth mindset is the key to both personal and professional success. The best part is that the growth mindset can be developed. Developing the growth mindset at work is also the key to developing high performance teams.

The growth mindset is an approach that spans boundaries across all the things we do, whether personal or professional. It is the same mindset at work whether we are doing something for fun or for a paycheck. The best way to cultivate the growth mindset is to use it for personal development. Everyone has some personal goals and ambitions. Use these ambitions to teach the growth mindset. Help employees develop personal development plans to achieve their personal goals. When you ask them what their personal development plans are, you might get lots of answers like, "I want to be a manager" or "I want to be promoted," and then a handful of employees might dare to say "I want to be a bestselling author" or "I want to make the world a better place." For those who want to progress their careers, ask them to craft a list of the skills and traits of an ideal person in that position, and ask them for their plans to master these skills. For those whose personal goals don't directly translate into work, encourage them to achieve their personal goals, and then bring the discipline and wisdom gained into the work setting. I encourage employees to discover bigger ambitions, dreams, and passions in life, and I push them to achieve their goals. No matter how different these goals are from work, there are many overlaps that grow people both personally and professionally. Most managers think that personal and professional lives are two different things and there should be clear boundaries between work and one's personal life. This view is somewhat skewed. A person going through a divorce cannot perform at his or her personal best. It is the same person, same brain, same aptitude, both at work and at home. Positive and negative experiences at either place affect the other. Encourage employees to develop on a personal or professional level, whichever they prefer. The growth in one will benefit the other.

Here is a simple technique I use to help my team discover their passions and ambitions:

> Step 1—Take a piece of paper and divide the paper into three equal parts using two lines.

> Step 2—Name the three individuals, dead or alive, whom you admire the most. These individuals do not have to be related to

your work. Write down these names in three separate columns on the paper.

Step 3—For each name, in each column, write three or more qualities you admire in these individuals. These should be qualities, not attributes like money, fame, or title.

Step 4—Analyze the overlap in qualities among these people. Highlight the similarities, including those that might influence or cultivate the related qualities.

Martin Luther King	Warren Buffet	My Father
1. Humanitarian	1. Long Term Thinker	1. Humble
2. Humble	2. Philanthropist	2. Humanitarian
3. Charismatic Leader	3. Hard Working	3. Patient

Self-Discovery Test Example

The overlapping qualities you highlighted are also your own personal qualities. To recognize readily traits in others, you must share a deep interest in those traits. These qualities may not be as developed in you, but recognizing your interest in these qualities is the first step toward developing them. Right now, you may not be recognized for those qualities or may not have accomplished as much as your idols, but if you follow your passion and develop these qualities, there is no limit to the amazing feats you can accomplish. The example I shared above is mine. I discovered through this exercise that I am passionate about humanity and I want to make a difference in the world. I brought that passion for humanity to work, which eventually led to creation of this program.

Solution Mindset—A solution mindset is a problem-solving approach that recommends that, no matter what the problem is, your first response should always be how to solve or get around the problem. In many ways, it is an extension of a growth mindset, but a solution mindset focuses more on how we react and respond when we encounter problems. Problems are an inevitable reality in life. Do you freeze or blame others for adversities, or do you try to figure out how to move forward?

Analyzing problems has its virtues. Identifying the cause of the problem helps us learn from our mistakes and avoid making the same mistakes in the future. Most modern management tactics have evolved from the industrial revolution, which placed heavy emphasis on problem analysis to minimize faults, increase production, and improve quality. Rigorous analysis of what, who, and why the problem occurred were critical in scaling operations without compromising quality. This practice was good for the industrial age where jobs were broken down into very specific, pre-defined tasks. Today's knowledge worker jobs, however, are a far cry from well-defined activities. Employees confront new challenges and have to solve problems they have never faced before. Employees have to make many novel decisions every day and analyzing problems for the root cause in such an environment causes more harm than good. When you ask questions like, "Who did it? Who is responsible for it? Why did it happen?" you train your employees to build protective boundaries around themselves. The prevailing leadership belief is that employees must be held accountable for poor decisions and punished for their wrongdoings. Yes, people should be held accountable for their actions, but only when those actions follow a repeated pattern. Otherwise, strict accountability starts to breed a culture of fault finding, finger pointing, and passing the blame. Employees then spend more energy building protective boundaries, safety nets, and political support than executing the task at hand. Employees become very risk averse and seek shelter under procedures and policies. Eventually, these procedures and policies become so strict that they become a barrier to productivity and creative problem solving.

A solution mindset, on the other hand, encourages progress. The goal is to keep moving forward. No matter what the problem is, focus on how to get around it and make progress. If all employees are constantly thinking of how to move forward, they are less likely to hide problems and waste resources covering up mistakes, defending their decisions, or looking for someone to blame. When everyone is focused on finding solutions, people attack the problem rather than the person, and collectively, they make sure the solution addresses the problem from all angles. In this type of environment, employees are more likely to bring problems to the group's attention and seek help. Many managers worry that if they don't analyze problems, the problems will keep recurring. In my experience, it is rare for a problem to repeat. The solution mindset often resolves most of the underlying problem without the added cost of analysis-paralysis.

To foster a solution mindset, tell employees that you are not interested in who or what caused the problem. You are only interested in hearing how we plan to go beyond the problem. This clarification forces them to think of solutions and take actions to make progress in spite of the problem's magnitude. For me, it completely changed the group's dynamics. In the beginning, a lot of employee performance and morale problems occurred, but soon, there were only technology problems. Today, I only hear about the problem when it is a technological limitation for which my team does not have an easy solution or when we need to deviate from the original plan. Problems are still prevalent, but they don't stop progress. I tell my team members, "You are the boss and you are the expert. This system is your baby, so you tell me how to address this." Often, I don't even have to say that anymore. They either take care of things, or they come to update me on the issues, or they consult with me on the approach.

Problems will occur, but solution-minded employees make progress knowing that problems will occur.

Partnership—American humorist Fred Allen said, "Treat employees like partners, and they act like partners." This philosophy is at the heart of the success of all the innovative companies cited in this book. This philosophy rebuilt Toyota in '40s, and it did the same for Starbucks in '90s. Starbucks calls its employees "partners," and in return, its partners have pushed Starbucks to be one of the top innovators in the world and one of the best places to work. In many ways, this philosophy is also the essence of this book. It is also my story and how the Bright Idea Box program came into existence.

Just like everyone else, after the 2008 economic downturn, I was facing challenges around budget cuts, staff reduction, and doing more with less. I tried many employee engagement techniques, but one particular technique caught on like wildfire. Inspired by Brasilata, I asked my team to help me come up with ideas to cut costs, improve departmental operations, and increase the level of service we provided. I am very blessed to have a great team. They came up with many ideas, ranging from small procedural changes to changing the technology platform to reduce maintenance costs. Building on these small successes, I started asking for ideas that could add value for the company and customers. Once again, my team did not disappoint me. One team member came up with the idea of "Electronic Signatures" after signing his home mortgage papers electronically; another employee suggested that we do away with mailing policy documents to customers after noticing that her auto insurance no longer sends the policy packet, which, as we know, gets shelved for a few months and later tossed in the garbage. The ideas kept rolling and my team was more engaged and excited than ever. Best of all, we implemented all of the ideas with no additional money or resources. Counter to the thought that because I had limited resources taking on these additional projects would reduce the quality of service, our service standards went up and users were more satisfied than ever.

If you want to get the best out of people, ask them for help rather than assigning them work. When you assign work, employees do the assigned work, but when you ask for help, they do whatever it takes to help you succeed. By slightly shifting your approach, you can dramatically improve the results. When employees see the effect of their work on the company's success, they are more committed and enthusiastic, and they take pride in everything they do.

I am very proud of my team, and I would like to claim that they are uniquely gifted, but the reality is that all employees want to do good work, be appreciated for the extra effort, and feel they are important. They are self-motivated when they see the effect of their work on the company's success. Sure enough, I saw similar results when I rolled out the program company-wide. I am confident that when you roll out this program, you will see similar results.

These basic leadership principles alone can transform employees into a highly productive workforce. Combine them with the innovation directive and you will have a highly engaged workforce that does excellent work and improves the business at the same time. Creating such a program can be a big change for some companies. In the next chapter, we will discuss some specific techniques to manage the changes this program brings and techniques for getting everyone onboard.

RECAP

- Lead with passion. Believe in your people. You can transform ordinary people into leaders who think and act like innovators.

- Four principles of higher engagement: Ownership, Personal Growth, Solution Mindset, and Partnership.

- Give people autonomy and ownership over their work. Ownership instills a feeling of pride and, as a result, people work much harder.

- Encourage employees to grow on a personal and professional level. Growth in one area benefits the other.

- Foster a solution mindset that emboldens employees to focus on finding solutions to problems, not the cause of the problems.

- Treat employees as if they are partners who have an important role that contributes to the organization's success.

Chapter Twelve Exercises

Q1. Who will be leading the Innovation Charter in your company?

_____

_____

_____

Q2. What are the current programs in place at your company that encourage employees to do more, learn new things, and want to grow?

_____

_____

_____

_____

_____

_____

Q3. What incentive programs does your company use right now? Can you list their purpose, how effective they are, and what kind of behavior they encourage?

_____

_____

_____

_____

_____

_____

Q4. What new programs can you implement that encourage employees to grow and learn?

_____

_____

_____

_____

_____

_____

Q5. What new techniques and programs can you employ to encourage managers to delegate and grow their direct reports?

_____

_____

_____

_____

_____

_____

Chapter 13

Managing Change

People don't resist change. They resist being changed.
— Peter M. Senge

For many, creating a bottom-up innovation program is a complete paradigm shift. It challenges many management practices and cultural norms. For years, the company may have operated under certain guidelines and a hierarchical structure in which managers are responsible for thinking up ideas for improvement and employee involvement is limited to execution. A program like the Bright Idea Box encourages employees to be bold and challenge existing practices, processes, management, and products. This very notion may make many leaders who have gotten used to having power and control uncomfortable. How do you create a program that runs against the tide? You may have inherited a dysfunctional culture or reached a critical inflection point where you feel the current culture is holding the company back. You are ready for change, but is your company ready?

Research shows that companies tend to follow the founders' values and management style. If the founders were innovative, the company also develops an innovative culture. If the founders had a strong focus on customer service, so does the company. If the founders were penny pinchers or focused on pocketing money for themselves, the company builds a culture of squeezing pennies out of customers and partners. I have witnessed this phenomenon in every company for which I have worked. If not challenged, these values tend to last long after the founders are gone. The good news is that these values are not set in stone. Companies reinvent themselves all the time. I bet you have many of your own stories of such transformations. Every adversity, business challenge, or market shakeup presents an opportunity to change the long engrained culture and norms. The bigger the adversity, the bigger the opportunity. Nothing mobilizes people, spurs action, and opens people to change more than a crisis. So never let a crisis go to waste.

Culture change is not an easy task. There is no project plan to follow and there is no finish date in sight. The lack of predictability and structure makes many leaders uncomfortable. Many simply give up and never set foot on this road. When the going gets tough, many find it easier to change jobs or replace employees than try to change the culture. Leading change is a skill set that most of us have never been trained on. Most leaders learn it the hard way. Occasionally, they get lucky and are able to hire outside help, but often, change is forced by economic crisis and there is no money to hire outside help. Then leaders are left to their own devices, which is perhaps also the number one reason why culture change efforts usually fail.

Leading change is a skill. Given how fast the business world is changing, change is becoming the norm. As Gary Hamel suggests in his book *The Future of Management*, "what distinguishes today's age is not the economic ascendance of China and India, not the degradation of our climate, not the resurrection of ancient religious animosities, but rather the frantic pace of change itself. What has changed is the change itself." If you don't change at the pace the world around you is changing, the change will be forced upon you and you will likely not be there to be part of the change. I strongly believe that leading change will be one of the most sought-after leadership skills in future leaders. Thankfully, it is a skill that you can easily learn.

Most people think that management is ready for change, but employees resist change. Every now and then, someone will confront me by saying, "It's easy for you to say it. You don't know what kind of people I have to deal with." Managers often feel that employees want to do the minimum and they won't change. Employees may agree to the change on the surface, but they go back to doing the same old things. Can you change these passive-aggressive people? The short answer is: Yes. Psychologists do it all the time. I am not suggesting that you become a psychologist, but just be mindful of the fact that changing people is possible. As a business leader, you can influence your employees in many ways that create a desire for change. You can create an environment that enables change and makes change a little easier.

People change all the time. The very people you think resist change happily undertake much larger changes in their lives. People get married, decide to have children, buy a house, change a lifestyle, change religious beliefs, quit smoking, move to a new location, and so on. These are much bigger changes than the changes you are asking of them. The difficulties you experience are often not the result of change, but rather the process used for change. The resistance comes more from dis-involvement in the decision-making process of the change than the change itself. The change is often imposed upon them. Often employees are not even aware of the reasons for change. Change comes in the form of a top-down mandate, instead of an inclusive rationale for change. Anytime you impose something on someone, you can be sure to expect resistance.

Resisting change is very human. We are biologically wired to resist change. Even those who say they are very open to change have to ponder over the change and its effects before they can accept it. Some may have a shorter turn-around cycle than others, but we all experience the same visceral, emotional response when we encounter change. I once attended a seminar on *Change Management*, which was supposed to be an in-person class, but at the last minute, the hosting organization changed the class set-up to be a mix of in-person and on the phone. I vividly remember this class because the instructor got upset because of this change. Here was a change expert, frustrated by the change.

Change forces us to do things differently, and whenever we do something differently, it requires our brain to focus and exert a lot more energy to complete the task. Our brain is a highly efficient machine, so it likes to exert as little energy as possible to do any task. Did you know that as you are reading these lines, your brain is predicting what the next word will be. We don't always read all the words, but rather look for patterns in words and sentences. You may recall your own incidents when you were reading aloud to someone and you said a different word than what was written. We are biologically designed to find the path of least resistance, and the least resistant path tends to be what we know. When we don't know something, we have to exert a lot of energy and we resent expending this energy, especially when the same results could have been achieved effortlessly.

We are creatures of habit, and changing habits requires a marriage of the rational mind and emotional drive. Jonathan Haidt, professor of psychology at the University of Virginia, captured the essence of how we change our habits in his book *The Happiness Hypothesis,* using the very powerful analogy of an elephant and its rider. Professor Haidt suggests that our emotional brain is like an elephant and the rational brain is like the rider. The rider seems to be the leader as it sits atop and holds the reins. But the rider is so small in comparison to the elephant that when the elephant wants to do something, the rider's power is no match for the elephant's. We can all relate to the power of the elephant when we give in to an urge, even when we know better. Whenever our change efforts fail, it is often the emotional elephant's fault, says Professor Haidt. Change is very emotional. It evokes fear. People are scared that they will not be able to perform the job at the level they did before. They are afraid that they will be judged and looked down upon. You need to be aware of this emotional resistance and make people comfortable with the change. For any long-term change to persist, it has to appeal to both the rational and emotional parts of the brain.

To launch the Bright Idea Box program, you need to appeal to the rational and emotional brains of three distinct stakeholders. First, the top management, the executive leadership team in the company. Second, the middle management layers, and third, the front-line employees. I recommend that you create distinct sales pitches for each group to address their functional needs.

Your first stop should be top management. If you are the CEO of the company, the authority vested in you makes it easier, but that does not mean that you do not need to spend energy convincing your team. You still need to sell the concept to them and get their buy-in. They have to feel that this program is going to help the company and their individual units. If you are a mid-level or senior manager, you will need to spend extra energy building the merit behind your recommendation. You can use this book and the examples I cited to make your case, or you can start an isolated effort just like I did. Once you have some success stories to share, you can push the program on a much broader level.

Start your sales pitch with your objectives and the program's potential benefits. Here's a list of potential benefits for reference:

- Increase Operational Efficiencies
- Improve Customer Satisfaction
- Identify Blind Spots and Inefficiencies
- Broaden the Customer Intelligence Gathering Network
- Align Products with Customers' Wants and Needs
- Increase Employee Engagement
- Increase Employee Retention
- Attract Top Talent

As you lay out your plans and the program's structure, invite members of management to help you tailor the program to better meet your company's needs. Remember, you don't want to impose the change; your goal is to make management part of the change. Increased participation creates a stronger buy-in and increases the chances of success. Once top management sees the list of benefits and how the program works, getting them on board will not be very difficult.

Once you have top management on board, your next challenge is to get middle managers and supervisors on board. Convincing this group will take a lot more effort than it did to convince the top management. The effort may vary widely depending on your organizational culture, layers of management, and what else is going on in the company. Nevertheless, you cannot bypass or ignore this group's importance. This group directly influences the line level employees' thinking and actions, so it can easily undermine your efforts if it is not on board. If the managers don't see the value that the program adds to them or how it makes their lives easier, you will have a hard time enticing employees to submit ideas. This group will ask a lot of questions about the program's credibility, how the program is going to work, and how it is going to affect the workload of already busy employees. Will it distract them from doing the real work? Don't be surprised if you find some of the middle management threatened by this initiative. This program empowers employees to bypass all the established channels of communication and authority, so they might fear losing their managerial power.

Once again, to get buy-in from this group's members, invite them to critique the program and help make it better. The most powerful selling point for this group might be the promise of reducing personnel issues, increased productivity, and getting managers out of the constant firefighting mode. I used the "Invisible Gorilla" experiment to stress to this group's members how they are busy juggling so many projects and dealing with conflicting priorities and other managerial responsibilities that they cannot spot production problems or suggest process improvements with so many other demands and pressures. Instead, they can use their employees as their eyes on the field. The Invisible Gorilla experiment was created by Christopher Chabris and Daniel Simons at Harvard University to show how focus creates cognitive blindness and why we miss seeing many things happening around us. We think we are seeing the world the way it is, but actually, we miss a lot of information. Our eyes see the information, but our brains do not process all the information, and therefore, it doesn't exist for us. If you are not familiar with the video, I recommend you stop reading now and search for "Invisible Gorilla" on YouTube (URL link: http://www.youtube.com/watch?v=vJG698U2Mvo). Follow the instructions on the screen. STOP READING NOW.... Go watch the video.

The video shows two teams, one wearing white shirts and the other wearing black shirts. The video instructs you to count how many times the players wearing white shirts pass the balls to their team mates. In the middle of the video, a person wearing a black gorilla suit passes through these players. Since everyone is so focused on the players with white shirts, hardly anyone notices the black gorilla. This video demonstrates how focus creates an unintentional blindness, which plays an important role in processing information and making decisions. Managers are constantly juggling priorities and processing a lot of information. They cannot see everything that is going on in the company. This video can help convey the point that managers need their staff to be on the lookout for ways to improve business functions and processes. The Bright Idea Box is an employee development tool that can help managers develop their direct reports by educating them on the basics of business decision making. Managers can use this program to redirect employees to focus on solutions and steer overly opinionated employees to stop complaining and develop ideas to solve the problem. Whenever these employees have an urge to complain, managers can ask them to suggest a solution and submit it as an idea. List as many selling points as you can so that mid-managers can see the benefits this program brings to them. If possible, recruit some managers and get them on board before making your pitch to the larger management group. Their enthusiasm and positive participation can help you get a stronger buy-in from the group.

The third stakeholder group is the employees. Getting employees excited about the program will not be difficult at all, but getting them to participate and generate ideas may take time. Most employees will be excited to have the opportunity to bring their ideas to life, make a difference, show off a little, and be recognized by management. However, they may not feel comfortable or safe submitting ideas that bring forward flaws in the system. Despite the fact that they don't need approval to submit an idea, most will gravitate toward running their ideas by their supervisors. You want them to collaborate with their supervisors to help them refine the idea, but you also need to be mindful that supervisors could suggest not pursuing an idea because it might make the employee look bad or reflect poorly on the manager or department. You will need to work with employees and managers to reduce this approval-seeking practice.

With the rollout of this program, you are asking employees to think and act differently—to do things in ways they have never done them before. Some might jump for joy while others might be in a bit of shock or disbelief. Dan and Chip Heath, in their book *Switch: How to Change When Change is Hard*, recommend the best way to make people comfortable with change is to share the things they are already doing that are needed for the change. Look for past employee-suggested ideas that were implemented at your company. Sharing these real life examples will make employees feel they have what it takes and they are capable of thinking like innovators. A famous car wash loyalty rewards experiment showed that the customer return rate increased by 82 percent when customers got a head start by receiving two stamps instead of one out of the ten stamps needed to earn a free car wash. The two free stamps made people feel they were 20 percent done already and well on their way to earning a free car wash. This encouraged them to return for more car washes. Stamp your employees' innovator card with ideas they have generated in the past. Look for examples they can relate to, especially the examples of ideas their fellow employees suggested. Stress the point that this program is designed to recognize employees for developing such ideas and they have already contributed valuable ideas. This program is there to recognize employees who otherwise don't get the credit they deserve.

If you are still unsure, or if the program looks risky for any reason, I recommend you start on a smaller scale. Learn from your own experiences; see what works and how to best tailor the program to meet your unique business and cultural needs. The successes in your own environment can help secure a stronger buy-in from all the stakeholders. That is how I started the program. I did not have many examples of companies in the service industry or a formula that I could follow that I was sure would work, so I created a very informal program at first. Once the program gained some momentum, I started to formalize it. With time, I became a believer and increasingly passionate about empowering employees to grow the business.

Once you have the buy-in from all layers of management, it is time to launch the program. In the next chapter, I will share some practical tips for launching the program and making a presentation to all employees.

RECAP

- The program could be a paradigm shift for many companies that have a hierarchical structure.
- To implement this program, you need buy-in from three distinct stakeholders: top management, middle management, and employees.
- Buy-in from middle management is challenging because management's role is to enforce processes and rules; therefore, managers might be the most resistant.
- Solicit input from each stakeholder group to refine the program and get a stronger buy in.
- Share past employees' ideas that are in use to build employee confidence.

Chapter Thirteen Exercises

Q1. How many layers of management do you have in your organization, and what kind of resistance do you expect from each, if any?

_____

_____

_____

_____

_____

_____

Q2. How many presentations do you need to do to convince each group, and what are the key selling points for each group?

_____

_____

_____

_____

_____

_____

_____

_____

_____

_____

Q3. Are there any individuals or business units who will be very excited about implementing this program?

_____

_____

_____

_____

_____

_____

Q4. Are there any business units or departments that might be resistant to this initiative, and what will be their primary objections?

_____

_____

_____

_____

_____

_____

Q5. What is your high level strategy for sharing information and convincing various stakeholders to implement this program? Do your best to prioritize so you talk to the most influential individuals first.

_____

_____

_____

_____

_____

_____

Chapter 14

Energizing Employees

The most powerful weapon on earth is
the human soul on fire.
— Ferdinand Foch

Inspiring employees requires an inspiring vision.

Rolling out the Bright Idea Box program to all employees is the most exciting part of the whole process. Now is when your speaking and motivational skills will be tested. Are you excited? Can you envision the cheers and the energy in the crowd? Can you get employees excited about the program's vision and their opportunity to be part of something larger than themselves? Can you light their souls on fire?

Don't worry; I am not asking you to become Tony Robbins or Deepak Chopra. I have outlined most of what you need to inspire your employees. All you have to do is follow the checklist I have outlined in this chapter and you will be surprised to discover the hidden motivational speaker inside you. That said, you do have to be comfortable with public speaking. You will have to stand in front of all employees repeatedly. This is not a one-time scripted speech. In your first presentation, you will be unveiling the program, and subsequently, you need to use every opportunity you can get to share stories and examples. You need to showcase the ideas generated by your employees and share case studies of other companies and how they innovated in a particular innovation domain. You will be refining the program, changing the rewards system, and celebrating ideas, so you better get comfortable with speaking. If you are not comfortable with speaking, I recommend you take a speaking course before launching the program. Speaking is an important leadership skill, and it is a good investment for your own career development.

Let's start from a very high level overview and then dive deeper into specific action items. The first success checklist is a review of what we talked about throughout this book. These are the specific highlights that you need to keep in mind as you start to prepare for the rollout.

SUCCESS CHECKLIST

✓ Define the need for innovation. Paint a picture that every employee can understand. Not the typical mission statement and not a bunch of tactics, but a higher-level goal that every employee can be proud of and use to validate his or her actions and decisions. Every time an employee takes on a task or project, he or she should be able to relate how it contributes to that bigger picture vision.

✓ Never lead with financial goals. Positive financial results are the outcome of achieving greatness, not vice versa.

✓ The program's objective is not innovation for innovation's sake, but rather for meaningful and measurable business results.

✓ Believe in your people and win employee backing.

✓ What's in it for employees? Present the program as an opportunity for employees to showcase their skills, get recognized, be promoted faster, and gain any financial rewards that you may decide to incorporate into the recognition process.

✓ Create an emotional connection. Consider how your company improves the lives of your customers and how your employees play a role in that.

✓ Provide assurance. Change can create fear among employees, especially automation and operational efficiency ideas. Assure them that the goal is not to put them out of work, but to advance both the organization and its employees. The workplace should be full of opportunities to do new things and to learn new skills.

✓ To maintain the purity of bottom-up innovation, only employees and first line managers/supervisors should be allowed to submit ideas. If higher-level management is allowed to submit ideas, employees will be intimidated and management's ideas will start to become directives rather than ideas that are up for discussion.

✓ If there is a business problem you want to address, make sure everyone sees it and experiences it. Bring people face to face with the challenge and give them the opportunity to help solve the problem.

✓ Don't inspire by numbers and corporate performance. Line level employees cannot easily relate to how their everyday actions affect corporate performance or financial balance sheets. They need simple examples of success and how their actions contribute to that success.

✓ Have a grand vision, but break it down to actionable items. No human being is capable of assimilating a grand design into his everyday activities. The action items need to be easily understood and easy to put into practice one by one.

✓ Design the program and consider all outcomes. And put your program into effect on day one: if an employee has a suggestion *about the program*, listen to it!

✓ Don't just announce a program and expect employees to read your mind. Communicate what you want and what you expect very clearly.

✓ Recognize employees for their contributions and create a culture that celebrates successes and likes to have fun.

The second checklist is a list of items you need to prepare before rolling out the program to all employees. Before you present the program to employees, you need to make sure that your Idea-Capturing System is ready and that you have the buy-in on all aspects of the program from all the affected parties. Here's a short list of items that must be in place before rolling out the program.

PRE-ROLLOUT CHECKLIST

- ✓ Get buy-in from all layers of management.
- ✓ Set up the Idea-Capturing System Website.
- ✓ Define and embed idea flow processes in the website.
- ✓ Name your website, for example: Idea Central or Idea Box.
- ✓ Post the purpose or mission statement document on the website.
- ✓ Document the incentive system and post it on the website.
- ✓ Post relevant links on the website: Videos, Books, Articles, Websites.
- ✓ Prepare material for at least a one-hour program rollout presentation.
- ✓ Purchase all props and recognition mementoes before launching the program.

As I shared earlier, we used pins for accepted ideas and I wanted pins that employees could tack outside their cubicles. Well, there are no tack pins on the market that symbolize ideas or innovation and are big enough to be seen easily. Additionally, most were for tacking on cloth, not cubicles. My IST members and I wasted many hours searching for something that would come close, but we found none. I had to have these custom-made and that took time. I am sharing this story only to make the point that this is a new field so you may not always find what you want easily. You may have to make compromises along the way. Also, keep in mind that seemingly trivial things like this will take time, but also that success can lie in attention to the details.

Once your tools and processes are in place, you need to prepare a one-hour presentation to give employees an overview of the program and how it works. In your presentation, you want to educate employees on what innovation is and how innovation goes beyond developing new products. Use examples from this book or search the Internet for companies that are more relevant to your business. Find examples that will resonate with your employees and company culture. Ask a lot of questions and keep your presentations as interactive as possible to engage employees. For example, you can ask questions like, "Can you name a few innovative companies?" and "What did they invent?" I embedded videos in my presentation. I used the "Did You Know?" video in my presentation to make the point that the world is changing very fast and we must keep up with its pace (YouTube link: http://www.youtube.com/watch?v=cL9Wu2kWwSY). It is a five-minute video that demonstrates the evolution of language, technology, the rate of adoption of newer innovations, and how the pace of change is affecting our lives. It is a good illustration for making the point that we cannot continue doing the same old things we have done for decades. We have to change and change fast. Employees must no longer be the passive recipients of management-enforced change, but rather the drivers of change. This program is designed to create a means for employees to become the catalysts of change. This understanding of change again reinforces why you need to innovate and innovate in a much broader sense than just developing new products.

PROGRAM LAUNCH PRESENTATION CHECKLIST

Here's the list of key items to cover in your presentation to all employees. This is a reference checklist. You should modify the list to make sure it addresses your program's unique features.

- ✓ Why is innovation important to the company?
- ✓ What role do employees play in the organization's success?
- ✓ How does this program present opportunities for employees?
- ✓ How do you define what innovation is?
- ✓ What are the domains of innovation, where you seek ideas?
- ✓ How do you transform an opinion into an idea?
- ✓ How do you look for ideas in everyday activities and sharpen innovation skills? (Addressed in Chapter Fifteen.)
- ✓ What is the function of the Idea Central website and what resources are available on the site?
- ✓ How do you enter ideas into the Idea Board?
- ✓ What is the process of idea implementation?
- ✓ What's in it for employees?
- ✓ What is the role of the Idea Support Team?
- ✓ How do you solicit interest to join the Idea Support Team?

You can also choose to save some elements of this information for another day. It might be too much information in one sitting for employees to digest. You can also choose to do a separate presentation on innovative thinking skills and give employees time to digest the information. They will be more receptive and prepared to absorb the message.

In the next chapter, we will discuss some very simple techniques that employees can use to discover new ideas. Practicing these basic innovation-thinking skills in everyday life and the work setting can transform average employees into innovators.

RECAP

- Prepare a 45 to 60 minute presentation for all employees that explains how the program works.

- Implement the Idea-Capturing System and purchase all the rewards and giveaways before the rollout.

- Sell the program to employees as a benefit and movement to empower employees.

- Share examples of ideas that employees can relate to so they will feel that they can come up with similar ideas.

- Explain the role of an Idea Support Team and solicit interest from employees to join the IST.

Chapter Fourteen Exercises

Q1. What do you need to complete before you deliver your presentation to all employees? Create the list of projects, milestones, and tasks that must be accomplished before rolling out the program.

_____

_____

_____

_____

_____

_____

_____

_____

_____

_____

_____

_____

_____

_____

_____

_____

Q2. Are you planning to share all of this information in one presentation or two (or more)? List each presentation title and the points you will be covering in each.

_____

_____

_____

_____

_____

_____

_____

_____

_____

_____

_____

_____

_____

_____

_____

_____

_____

_____

_____

_____

_____

_____

Chapter 15

Developing Innovation Skills

Every child is born an artist; the problem is to
remain an artist once we grow up.
— Pablo Picasso

Innovation thinking is a way of life. It is a lifestyle.

Humans are natural explorers. Curiosity and learning is in our
DNA. Most of us derive great pleasure from solving problems and
doing novel things. Some of us may have lost that curiosity and
creativity along the way, but the good news is that it can be easily
relearned. Innovative thinking stems from a creative problem-
solving mindset. Creativity in a business context is simply thinking up alternative ways of doing something. According to a recent
Harvard study, creativity is 85 percent a learned behavior. This is
great news for those of us who don't feel creative.

Innovative thinking is a skill. Those who have already mastered
this skill appear to spit out innovative ideas like a plastic molding
machine. Those who have not developed these skills are awestruck

by these people's ability to generate ideas and see beyond the curve. But, it is just like any other skill; when we are not good at a skill, it seems very difficult and we wonder how do others do it. It's simply a matter of practice. With practice, anyone can generate ideas and build the skills to differentiate good ideas from not so good ones.

In 2011, three professors, Jeff Dyer from Brigham Young University, Hal Gregersen from INSEAD, and Clayton Christensen from Harvard University, published the book *Innovator's DNA: Mastering the Five Skills of Disruptive Innovators.* The book is based on their eight-year study of the world's most respected innovators, including Steve Jobs, Richard Branson, Jeff Bezos, and Mark Benioff. They were interested in how these innovators find so many disruptive innovation ideas and whether these skills can be developed. I highly recommend reading this book to polish your personal innovation skills and bring out the innovator inside of you.

I have compiled a short list of skills that you can share with employees when you roll out the program. This is by no mean a comprehensive list of skills or techniques, but rather a starting point and enough to jump-start employees' innovative thinking abilities. It is a short list that employees can easily understand and put to use immediately.

CURIOSITY

Curiosity is perhaps the most imperative trait of all innovators. Being curious about what is on the other side and why things are the way they are is a great tool for making breakthrough discoveries. Most people accept the rules as they are and never question who came up with these rules and why they were created to begin with. Many people complain about products, processes, or systems, but they rarely ask why they were created this way or why they work this way. Questioning norms can lead either to better understanding or to devising a new way of doing business. Curiosity prompts learning, and continuous learning is essential for innovative thinking. Often the best ideas come from learning about something that has been in use in one setting and applying it to another.

Ask curious questions like, "Why?" "Why not?" and "What if?" to start the idea conversation. Encourage everyone to ask questions like, "Why are we doing it this way?" "Why don't we do it the way the auto industry does it?" and "What if we added a feature like this?" Children are very good at asking "why" and "why not" questions. If you have kids, pay attention to their questions. You will be amazed by their curiosity and you can learn a lot from the kinds of questions they ask. Bringing that childlike curiosity to work can significantly boost your creative thinking. Most people don't ask questions because they are afraid that they will look stupid in front of others. Trying to keep up appearances, they never discover anything new. Now, mind you, I said bring childlike curiosity to work, not the behavior.

Velcro is a great example of curiosity and asking "what if" questions. The inventor of Velcro, George de Mestral, was returning from a hunting trip in the Swiss Alps. He was annoyed by the burrs his dog had picked up during the trip. Not only was removing the burrs time-consuming, but they were so annoyingly sticky that they stuck to almost anything, including his clothes. George's frustration spurred his curiosity until he decided to look at the burrs under a microscope. To his surprise, he found burrs were covered with hundreds of tiny hooks that caught on to anything with loops. Nature had blessed the Burdock plant with an evolutionary design to spread its seeds by sticking to animal fur. George did not stop there; he questioned, "What if I created burr-like hooks? Could they be used for attaching things?" George's curiosity led to the development of Velcro, an alternative to the zipper. George's curiosity, his questioning why burrs were so sticky, inspired him to develop an iconic product.

LISTENING

Customers are always telling us what they want, but employees on the other end are often not listening. There is no incentive for them to put up with customer complaints all day. As a result, companies end up losing golden opportunities to know their customers and learn what they really want. To get the best ideas, you need to train your employees to observe: Why do customers call? When do they call? Are they happy to talk to you, or are they frustrated that they had to call you? Pay attention to their requests. Tuning-in to your customers' requests—and yes, their complaints' can generate insights that will align your products with what customers really want.

Surveys and other customer feedback mechanisms are excellent tools for collecting customer insights, but everyday employee interactions are much more powerful than the deliberate exercise of thinking up wants and needs. Starbucks' two percent milk idea was a cornerstone idea that emerged out of active listening. Starbucks created a culture that promotes listening to customers for ideas. After noticing that customers were repeatedly asking baristas for low fat milk, Starbucks allowed customers to choose the type of milk they preferred in their lattes. This seemingly insignificant idea radically transformed Starbucks and put the company on a steep trajectory of growth.

Train your employees to pay attention to what customers are saying and look for ideas to enhance your products. Ritz-Carlton trains its employee to observe customers for verbal and non-verbal cues. Any time a customer makes a request or suggests something, Ritz employees fill out an incident form, which goes into the guest history database. Ritz uses this database to serve the individual needs of guests and analyze how their products and services meet the needs of customers. You should also develop a database of customer insights and needs to figure out what your customers value.

Consider IKEA's new loading and delivery service. The idea emerged from a frequent complaint, "How do I load all this heavy furniture into the truck?" Now its website offers this:

With our fantastic new Picking with Delivery service, we do all the heavy lifting for you! Now, shopping is as easy as 1-2-3!

1. Visit your local IKEA store and see one of our co-workers.

2. Tell the co-worker what you're looking for and they'll create and print an itemized list of your items.

3. Take your list to the checkout area and pay for your purchase. Then, proceed to our delivery area where you can arrange for home delivery.

We'll get your products and have them delivered starting at just $99! It's that easy!

IKEA is full of such innovations, from onsite daycare to replenishing your battery with non-fat frozen yogurt at the end of your shopping trip. Listening to your customers is perhaps the best way to align your products with what customers want. When products are aligned with what customers want, people line up to buy these products. You may have seen or heard about this phenomenon in action outside Apple stores.

MINING

Every frustration presents an opportunity. Instead of getting frustrated and blaming others for incompetence, mine your frustrations to look for ways to solve the problem. How would you handle the problem if you were in the other person's shoes? What would you do differently? Is it an expectations problem or a systemic problem? Do you have a better way to handle the same situation or thoughts on how to avoid the problem altogether? You don't always have to have solutions. Solutions might come to you after the fact or by asking other people in your network to help you come up with a solution. The more important piece is to have a mindset that is always thinking of how to turn frustrations into opportunities.

Use the same technique for customer frustrations. What frustrated the customer? Is there a pattern of similar frustrations? How can you eliminate or reduce that frustration? Can you change some internal process or system to solve the problem? Is this a customer training or awareness problem? Can you develop some videos or "how to" content to educate customers?

Finding opportunities in frustration is a key quality of innovators. Innovators don't blame others; they look for ways to solve the problem or get around the problem. Out of this solution-oriented approach, they get new ideas for solving problems that sometime end up completely changing the business world. Going back to IKEA's origin again, the self-assemble furniture idea emerged out of an employee's frustration with trying to load the furniture back into the truck. Removing the legs of the table did the trick, and he wondered whether customers experienced the same problem. Not all furniture needs to be delivered and assembled at customers' homes by specialists. Not to mention the storage and transportation costs.

Frustrations are often the best source of new ideas. Some of the best innovations and most successful startup companies have emerged out of frustrations. Scott Cook developed Quicken Software after observing his wife's frustrations with managing personal finances and staying on top of paying bills. Scott developed simple software to consolidate bills and balance checkbooks for his wife. He came to find out that billions of people across the globe shared the same frustration, and many now use Quicken to manage their finances. eBay is another child of similar frustrations. Pierre Omidyar's girlfriend expressed frustration around finding likeminded people on the Internet who would be interested in trading Pez dispensers. Eager to help and impress his girlfriend, he developed an online auction website, which very quickly became the leading trading platform for all kinds of specialty collectors. Today, you can sell almost anything on eBay. Some of the most innovative and successful companies around the world, like W.L.

Gore, SalesForce.com, and the Virgin brand of companies were born out of turning frustrations into opportunities.

Keeping a positive attitude is essential to finding opportunities in frustrations. Ask yourself, "How do I react when I run into a problem?" Do you get frustrated and look for the cause or do you look for alternatives. We are innately programmed to look for the cause of the problem so we can avoid repeating the same mistake, and unfortunately, we end up spending more time finding the cause of the problem than solving the problem. Accept setbacks, failures, and adversities as part of life, and cultivate a solution mindset. Whenever you are faced with a challenge, ask yourself, "How can I get around the problem?" Focus on the bigger picture and always look for solutions. Here are five essential traits to follow in pursuit of building a solution mindset:

1. Not stopping at the first obstacle

2. Keeping a positive attitude

3. Always learning

4. Collaborate—share and ask for help

5. Solution finding rather than complaining

BORROWING

We like to believe that our problems are unique, but more often they are not. Often the problems we are wrestling with have been solved by others in different industries and in different products. Steve Jobs found the inspiration and solution of rounded corners for the Mac case in Cuisinart kitchen appliances. Look for inspiration from the outside world. You will be amazed to find how many products have already solved the problems you might be struggling with. Pick up your favorite product and try to decode how this product or the maker of the product has solved the same problem. If you are looking for truly breakthrough ideas, go out into nature. Nature is one of the most rapidly growing sources of inspiration in innovation. More and more scientists are turning to nature for ideas. One Japanese engineer solved the sound blast problem of ultra-fast bullet trains when they entered tunnels by noticing how a kingfisher dives into the water without making a splash.

Henry Ford was a true innovator who revolutionized the auto industry. Ford's Model T was a disruptive innovation that used many new innovations like an alloy frame and body, one piece engine block, removable cylinder heads, and flexible suspensions, but what turned the Model T into an icon in manufacturing was its assembly process. Henry Ford did not invent the assembly line; he borrowed the idea from a meat packing plant. Ford saw how Armour and Swift meat packing plants in Chicago had revolutionized the process of mass production through a series of disassembly and assembly steps and decided he wanted to use the same technique for assembling cars. Despite all the new innovations, Ford managed to produce much cheaper cars, and more of them, because of the assembly line. And all thanks to a borrowed idea from a meat packing plant.

When Apple created the iPod, the MP3 player that could hold a thousand songs, the large collection of music created a new problem: How to navigate to song number eleven on the eightieth album? The traditional approach had been to navigate to the desired song using forward and backward buttons. Apple realized that nobody was going to be happy clicking ninety-one times to get to his or her favorite song. One of the Apple engineers working on the iPod design team was playing with the number lock when it suddenly came to him. Why not build a wheel-like interface that would allow the user to navigate without clicking? The scroll wheel lets users navigate faster by dialing it faster or slower, depending on how far down the list they want to go. The engineer associated the experience of navigating through numbers on a number lock to navigation of music on the iPod.

NETWORKING

The most innovative ideas often lie at the intersection of two different paths. We get some of the best ideas when we network with people from different disciplines. As Steve Jobs mentioned in his 2005 commencement speech at Stanford, if he hadn't dropped in to take a calligraphy class at Reed College, the world of computing might not have had the wonderful typography that it does. However, you don't need to go take art classes to discover new possibilities. Network with peers from different departments, backgrounds, and interests and you will get a new perspective on how others look at similar problems or solve similar challenges. Our natural inclination is to stay within our confinements and network with people with similar backgrounds and interests. This means everyone in your network thinks and acts the same way. You never get a new perspective on how to solve the problem or new ideas on how to do things completely differently. Sometimes, people in different disciplines have a solution to your problem and sometimes you have a solution to their problems.

Kevin Dunbar, a renowned psychologist, studied thousands of hours of tapes of various scientists at work to figure out how and when they get breakthrough ideas. His research revealed that the best ideas don't come when scientists are working hard at their bench, but rather in lab meetings where all the scientists are sharing their discoveries and mistakes. Hearing others' successes and failures triggered associations.

Thomas Edison is one of the most celebrated inventors of all time. People picture Edison working alone in a lab, in a white coat, hunkered down, playing with circuits, and suddenly "poof" the light bulb idea hit him. The reality couldn't be any farther from truth. Edison had a large team working for him. Edison was a genius, but he was also a master collaborator. Most of the scientists of his time were introverts who placed higher emphasis on pure science than the application of science. Edison, on the other hand, was outgoing and entrepreneurial-minded. It wasn't until he moved to New Jersey and started networking with people from other disciplines that he started producing groundbreaking inventions.

If you want truly breakthrough ideas, network with people from completely different backgrounds. A left brain heavy engineer can learn a great deal from a right brain artist. If you are not ready to be that daring, just start by networking with people from different departments.

WRITING

The common understanding is that ideas come to us when we are in a relaxed state, going about doing mundane things, and suddenly it hits us. Bam! The solution to our problem. Ideas often come when we are not looking. This is because of how our brain works. Our cognitive brain, which is responsible for decision making, has a limited capacity to process information, but our intuitive brain, which works in the background, can process a lot more information and make new associations that trigger aha moments. But that does not mean if you stop looking for solutions, the solutions will come to you. Ideas come to us because we are looking for solutions. Even though our cognitive brain may not have been processing information, our intuitive brain is constantly processing information and making associations. To get ideas, you have to be looking for ideas. The second limitation of our cognitive brain is its ability to convert short-term memory into long-term memory. Often we get ideas, but they get lost in the rush of a million other things to do and remember. For this reason, recording problems and thoughts is essential to generating ideas.

The world's most creative and innovative thinkers, from Leonardo Da Vinci to Thomas Edison, were in the habit of keeping hundreds of journals of ideas. Thomas Edison filled more than 3,500 notebooks with sketches and illustrations of ideas. Any time a thought or idea crossed his mind, he wrote it down. Ideas don't always come fully formed either. They often arrive in small bits and pieces. The most innovative ideas are not any one thought, but a cross-fertilization of different thoughts. Our cognitive brain thinks in a very linear way, so we look at the problem from the most obvious and straightforward angle. We often get stuck because the answer lies in non-routine practice. Then the solution emerges when you are not thinking of that particular problem, but rather a different problem. As you are contemplating solutions to the new problem, one of those solutions hits as a potential solution to another problem. If you have written down the earlier problem, it allows you easily to go back to the problem where you left off. If you haven't, you need to reconstruct the problem, which presents the danger of getting stuck in the original linear thinking again. This is why all the innovative geniuses kept hundreds of notebooks.

Your writing tool does not have to be a notebook. It could be anything that lets you record and easily retrieve ideas. I record my thoughts on my cell phone, on my voice recorder, and in the notebooks that I keep in the car, office, and by my bedside. You never know when you will have the urge to sketch out an idea. The more accessible the tools, the more likely you will use them. This entire book was written that way.

PROBLEM SOLVING

Innovative solutions are not always about coming up with ideas for new things to do. Often you need innovative solutions for the challenges you are facing. Here are a handful of techniques you can teach employees for problem solving.

Asking "Why" Five Times

Asking why five times is one of my favorite techniques for discovering the root cause of a problem. This approach suggests that you ask "why" five times. Don't try to look for solutions for the first why, but rather the fifth why, which is often the root cause of the problem. It is best described in this 2006 statement from Toyota. The message refers to Taiichi Ohno, former executive vice president of Toyota Motor Corporation and the pioneer of the Toyota Production System in the 1950s.

> We come across problems in all sorts of situations in life, but having no problems is the biggest problem of all. Ohno saw a problem not as a negative, but, in fact, as a *kaizen* (continuous improvement) opportunity in disguise. Whenever one cropped up, he encouraged his staff to explore problems first-hand until the root causes were found. "Observe the production floor without preconceptions," he would advise. "Ask 'why' five times about every matter."

> To demonstrate the usefulness of his method he used the example of a welding robot stopping in the middle of its operation. The root cause of the problem was discovered through persistent enquiry:

> 1. "Why did the robot stop?"—The circuit has overloaded, causing a fuse to blow.
>
> 2. "Why is the circuit overloaded?"—There was insufficient lubrication on the bearings, so they locked up.
>
> 3. "Why was there insufficient lubrication on the bearings?"—The oil pump on the robot is not circulating sufficient oil.
>
> 4. "Why is the pump not circulating sufficient oil?"—The pump intake is clogged with metal shavings.
>
> 5. "Why is the intake clogged with metal shavings?"—Because there is no filter on the pump.

> The solution? Install a filter on the oil pump.

REVERSING THE CHALLENGE

I have sat in many brainstorming meetings throughout my career where the group is dancing around the problem but not addressing it. It could be the group-think syndrome or fear of not wanting to be the first one to challenge authority. The entire group is throwing out suggestions for adding new features to entice customers, but no one is addressing the real problem as to why customers are not buying in the first place. The best technique to overcome this challenge is to look for ways to solve the reverse of the problem, also known as opposite problem solving.

Let's say you are trying to think of ways to improve customer service. Instead of asking for ideas to improve your customer service, ask how you can win the "worst customer service" award. To make it even more distant, you can ask how your competitor can win that award. List all the things that will tick customers off so they never want to do business with that entity again. This technique can help you overcome the blank-sheet syndrome and generate a list of things that really matter to customers. Score each item on the list on a scale from one to ten, with ten being the top customer repellent. Take the top items, with a score of seven and higher, and evaluate how your company performs based on each of these items. If your customers had to rate your products on these items, with one being the worst and ten being the best, how would your customers rate these services? For anything less than ten, find out what you need to do to turn the item into a ten.

PROTOTYPING

Prototypes are excellent conversation starters. A prototype is a rough version of the product or the thought that lets others get a better feel for your intentions. It takes the thought out of your head and puts it into a real, tangible thing. It minimizes translational errors. Prototypes are almost mandatory for new product development, but prototypes can be useful in a wide range of settings. A prototype does not have to be a fully developed sample product. It could be anything, ranging from a hand-drawn sketch to a fully developed product, and anything in between. The latter just mean a better prototype. People don't think of drawings as prototypes, but actually they are simply an early stage of a prototype. An illustration of the process flow, hierarchy of actions, or cause and effect can communicate points much more effectively than a long description. As the common saying goes, "A picture is worth a thousand words." Use drawings, cardboard pieces assembled using duct tape, Play-Doh, clay putty, and other materials as much as possible to convey your ideas. You will get more constructive feedback and detect problems early in the process. When you cannot develop a prototype, try testing your idea on a handful of customers first. Collect feedback and refine the product as much as possible before rolling it out to the masses.

You want employees to exercise these skills every day. You need to make a deliberate effort to train employees. You can send them to training classes or bring outside experts to help them develop these skills. If you cannot afford to send all employees to training, look for online classes they can attend. If your budget does not allow, simply share the examples and stories I have outlined in this chapter. Just bringing these concepts to your employees' attention will significantly boost their innovative thinking.

RECAP

- Innovation thinking skills can be learned.

- Encourage employees to be curious and ask a lot of questions.

- Train employees on active listening skills and encourage employees to listen to customers for ideas.

- Foster a solution mindset in the entire organization that encourages employees to look for ways to turn frustrations into opportunities.

- Use the Idea-Capturing System as a means for recording observations and ideas.

- Create opportunities for employees to network with peers from other business units.

Chapter 16

Taking It to the Next Level

Ideas are like rabbits. You get a couple and learn how to
handle them, and pretty soon you have a dozen.
— John Steinbeck

Let me be honest and admit that moving the masses is not easy.
It takes time, patience, and perseverance.

You may have spent months trying to convince all layers of
management, then creating an innovation program that perfectly
fit your organizational mission and culture. You delivered a moving
speech that wowed employees and made them jump for joy. Your
program is now officially live. But ideas are nowhere in sight.

Don't panic.

I know that it is very painful to comprehend that you created
a perfect opportunity for employees to be recognized, voice their

ideas, and stand out from the crowd, but there is very little traction. Employees are not stampeding to jump on this golden opportunity.

Unfortunately, this is Newton's Law in action—"An object at rest stays at rest and an object in motion stays in motion." It takes a lot of energy to get the wheels turning. Jim Collins, in his book *Good to Great*, uses the analogy of a flywheel to demonstrate that every business change requires a lot of energy in the beginning, but it gets easier once you have momentum. Getting a flywheel started takes a lot of energy—you push, and you push, and you push. Then with every turn, it becomes easier and easier to turn the wheel. And finally, it starts to generate its own momentum and what once took an enormous amount of energy becomes almost self-sustaining. It is the same for starting a bottom-up innovation program. It is a cultural shift and you will need to make a really strong push in the beginning and keep pushing until it gains momentum. With time, the recognition and the buzz created by this program will create a desire among employees to submit ideas. Pretty soon, you will have ideas pouring in at a speed faster than you can handle. The key is not to stop pushing.

Most of the ideas submitted in the beginning will not be very innovative or have any pizzazz. These ideas will range from small process improvements, minor systems enhancements, and lots and lots of self-centered ideas that make one or a handful of individuals' lives easier at the expense of others. This is when you will be thankful that you asked employees to develop a business case for their ideas. Despite asking all the clearly spelled out questions, you will still get plenty of ideas with no thought as to who will benefit from this idea, how people will benefit, what is the magnitude of the problem or the solution, how to solve the challenge, and above all, whether it is even worth spending any time or money to solve this problem. In the early months of the program, the ideas will be a mixed bag of opinions and ideas.

For many employees, the world begins and ends with their jobs; therefore, improving their job functions will mean a lot to them. At times, you will have to reject some ideas and let the employees know that in the bigger scheme of things, their ideas do not add value, or the cost of the solution outweighs the benefits. It is very hard to reject ideas when you don't have a whole lot of ideas and you also don't want to discourage employees. On the other hand, this situation is also an excellent opportunity to educate employees. But be careful how you go about educating them. When you tell an employee that his idea was not accepted, he will not be very open to hearing a lecture on how to develop better ideas. Try to break the rejection and education into two separate meetings. You also constantly have to remind employees to keep customers in mind when submitting ideas.

FOCUS ON LITTLE IMPROVEMENTS

Everyone wants to develop the next iPod. But do you have hundreds of millions of dollars to experiment with? Can you afford such risks? Apple spent $350 million on Newton, which was a complete failure. It taught Apple a valuable lesson, and thankfully, Apple still had some money left to experiment and develop the iPod. Can you imagine if Apple had burnt through all of its R&D cash on Newton? Be mindful of the lure of large markets and grand ideas. Big ideas also carry big risks.

When people hear the word "innovation," what comes to every-one's mind are successful multimillion-dollar products. Why is it that no one thinks of a humble wire hanger as innovation? If that doesn't register on your innovation meter, how about the idea of sticking foam on a wire hanger so your clothes won't slip? All the women reading this book can appreciate this idea, and its inven-tor made millions from a less than $10 experiment. Innovation does not have to be a grandiose product, but something that adds value for consumers or solves a problem. If you dive deeper into the history of mega-success products, you will find that they are all a collection of small innovations built over time.

As a company grows and starts to deal in billions of dollars, it creates a culture that often ignores or undervalues the impor-tance of small wins because the profits are not large enough to attract corporate resources. New ideas tend to have low profits, and often the prospects for profit appear very small in the beginning. But as Clayton Christensen demonstrated in his book *Innovator's Solution*, if you don't pay attention to little stuff, new entrants will start to eat your profits from the low end of your market tier and keep climbing upwards until they put you out of business.

Sweat the small stuff; it pays off a lot more than you may think.

TAKE BABY STEPS

One of the biggest temptations is to set financial goals for the innovation program. Your baby hasn't even crawled yet, but you want her to be an Olympian. If you are just starting out in building an innovative culture, you have a long way to go before you can tie financial goals to the innovation program. Avoid setting arbitrary goals like the number of new ideas per year or financial results of new innovations. You need to emphasize the quality of ideas, not the quantity. That difference is a very hard pill to swallow for many business leaders, but if you are expecting a cultural shift, you need to pull the reins on your left brain and use your right brain to create a culture of innovation for long-term success.

Financial goals work best for short sprints, but not for long-term behavioral changes. If and when you feel ready to set goals, try to set goals that measure business metrics like customer satisfaction, ease of doing business, lower cost by a certain value, or eliminating waste by a certain percentage, which employees can relate to in their day-to-day activities. Employees can rarely relate to financial metrics that excite Wall Street investors or the top management. They don't know how to read financial balance sheets, and they often feel removed and distant from these metrics. So they leave it to management to take care of financials and keep doing what they have always done. Financial results are the outcome of good work. Financial goals don't necessarily encourage good behavior, quite the contrary.

KEEP REFINING THE PROGRAM

In the early days, you will have very few ideas, but as time progresses, the ideas will start flowing in at a pretty fast pace. There is a possibility that the IST will become the bottleneck in reviewing the number of ideas flowing in or the supporting departments will not have enough resources to implement all the ideas. As the program matures, you may want to consider increasing the number of IST members, or creating multiple committees based on business functions or geographies. You will also have to start pushing business case development down to the employees by asking more specific questions like "Who will be affected during and after the implementation?" "How many customers will benefit from this idea?" "How do we test the idea?" and "What is the true cost of implementation?" You can also push employees to develop prototypes before bringing ideas to the committee for more resources.

If you are not getting enough ideas, you may want to consider instituting "experimentation time." You can start very small, like a half-day a month or one day a quarter. This will force employees to spend some time thinking of new ideas. Give them the freedom to choose if they want to participate and when and how they want to use this time. Depending on their workloads and roles, they can use the entire chunk of time in one go or break it down into smaller increments. If possible, create a special place in the office where employees working on their "experimentation time" can go to work, network, and exchange ideas with others.

Keep soliciting feedback from employees to refine your idea questions, processes, and rewards based on the feedback, momentum, and the flow of ideas.

HIRE FOR MINDSET

In the beginning, you are trying to lift the mindset of your current employees and get the program off the ground. Once the program is refined to the point that it works for your company and you have plenty of ideas to showcase, shift your focus to training and hiring for the right mindset. Brasilata makes its new employees sign an innovators pledge, which states that they will look for ideas to improve the company and add value for customers. They stamp the "innovator" identity on all employees and employees do their best to uphold that standard. For your future hires, give them an overview of your program and ask them to give examples of innovative work they have done in the past. This program is an excellent recruiting tool. List it on your website where all future hires can see it. Employees want to work for employers who value their input and treat them as partners in success.

Celebrate successes and create a culture of fun.

Your Action Plan

You can't cross the sea merely by standing
and staring at the water.
— Rabindranath Tagore

Now that you have read this book, I would like you to take action to implement this program. You have spent some time and energy reading this book. Don't let it go to waste. More and more companies are realizing that they need programs that engage employees and grow the business. Soon such programs will be as ubiquitous as 401Ks and health benefits. If you do not create an environment that engages employees on a higher level, they will leave to join other companies that do. This is particularly true for knowledge workers whose base salaries are high enough that money and other tangible benefits like 401Ks and health insurance become increasingly less of a motivator.

Companies that fail to tap into employees' inner desires to be recognized, appreciated, and be part of something larger, suffer from adverse selection, where highly talented and self-motivated employees leave to pursue other jobs and companies are left with second grade employees. These companies also fail to attract good new talent. When new hires are evaluating job offers, they naturally gravitate toward the employer who treats its employees like partners, likes to have fun, and celebrates individual employee contributions. Smart and talented employees are not motivated by money or safety, but rather respect, identity, and a desire to grow.

Now I want you to write your next action steps and a detailed plan to implement this program at your company. Use the space below to craft a strategy and outline your tactics. Refer to the questions you answered at the end of each chapter to help you get started. If you need help or guidance in getting started or convincing management, email me at Jag@IdeaEmployee.com.

_____

_____

_____

_____

_____

_____

_____

_____

_____

_____

_____

_____

_____

_____

_____

_____

_____

_____

_____

_____

_____

_____

_____

_____

_____

_____

_____

_____

_____

_____

_____

_____

_____

_____

_____

_____

Appendix A

Case Studies

3M

3M is the founder of the concept of giving employees dabble time. Did you know that 3M is an abbreviation for Minnesota Mining and Manufacturing Company? That's right. 3M was a sandpaper making company that was struggling to survive after the mining industry hit the bottom. In 1923, Richard Drew, one of the engineers at 3M, saw a painter struggling to mask one section to paint a two-tone car. Drew was confident that his company could solve the painter's problem. Despite pressure from the top, Drew did not give in and ultimately found the right backing paper after two years of struggle. The product became known as Scotch tape, and it made millions for 3M. Management quickly realized the power of letting engineers follow their instincts and officially launched its 15 percent program to encourage experimental doodling. 3M's well-known Post-it Note is one of the hundreds of products that has come out of this 15 percent dabble time program. The program transformed 3M from a struggling, small company to a Fortune 500 company.

ATLASSIAN

Atlassian is a software development company that develops software tools for project collaboration and defect tracking software. To increase employee engagement and make sure software developers were having fun at work, the company decided to allow developers to work on any problems they wanted. The developers were given twenty-four hours, and after the twenty-four-hour period, they had to show their ideas to the company. They called this exercise the "FedEx Days." This offbeat exercise produced so many great ideas and fixes to lingering problems that Atlassian decided to turn it into a quarterly event, eventually leading to its policy of dedicating 20 percent of employees' time to experimentation and doing non-routine work.

BRASILATA

Brasilata is a steel can manufacturing company located in Brazil. Inspired by Japanese automakers' Total Quality Management process, Brasilata decided to engage its front-line employees to compete in a very mature and saturated industry. The company launched a program called *Projeto Simplificacao* (the simplification project), which encourages all of its 900 or so employees to think up as many incremental improvement ideas as possible. The transformation was remarkable. As a result, Brasilata has been ranked among the top twenty innovative companies in Brazil and has won many prestigious awards, including Sherwin-Williams' "Best Packaging Supplier," as well as "the best place to work" in Brazil. Brasilata receives more than 200,000 ideas per year and some of the small incremental improvements have turned into big innovations. Brasilata makes its new hires sign an innovation contract, which states that they will be on the lookout for ideas at all times. It refers to its employees as innovators, and having that title inspires employees to work hard to live up to it.

GOOGLE

Google gives all of its employees 20 percent time to work on their pet projects. Employees choose ideas and teams they would like to work on and are rewarded handsomely for ideas that get integrated into the Google suite of services. In addition, Google has created a 70-20-10 model, in which it dedicated 70 percent of its resources to its core product offerings, 20 percent to adjacent products that support or closely align with its core products, and 10 percent to new experimental products. Google has its own idea tracking system, which tracks different new products people are working on and serves as a tool for attracting team members who might be interested in joining the team. All ideas that have passed the initial feasibility phase are deployed to a handful of users for beta testing. Based on the response from the Beta community, founders can make the case to get further funding and support to take the product to the next level.

RITZ-CARLTON

Ritz-Carlton is famous for its world class service and its service is founded on treating employees like partners. Its unique partnership culture starts with the motto: "We are ladies and gentlemen serving ladies and gentlemen." Ritz has built a systematic framework for observing and recording ideas to provide the absolute best service. Ritz trains its employees to observe the environment and interact with guests to find their preferences, special needs, likes and dislikes, and emotional responses to various services. If the cleaning staff notices that you have used the entire box of tissues, the staff will not only put extra tissues in your room, but it is also noted in the guest history system to ensure that you have extra tissues during your next stay. The company permits its employees to spend up to $2,000 on any single guest per incident to make sure that guest is satisfied. Ritz employees observe their guests to come up with ideas to improve the facilities based on guest experience, reactions, and locale needs.

TOYOTA

Toyota was the first company to challenge established industrial management practices by treating its employees as intelligent human beings and not as a specialized task force with a limited view of the world and knowledge of the business. In 1951, Toyota launched the creative idea suggestion system to improve quality, minimize waste, and foster agility. This system of participation and engagement has made Toyota an icon of quality and the number one automaker in the world. It is estimated that Toyota's global workforce has contributed more than 40 million ideas. Toyota has kiosks deployed throughout the plant so employees at the assembly line can submit ideas when they are fresh in their minds. Toyota Production System is also the most studied and replicated management system and its impact has gone way beyond the manufacturing industries.

WHOLE FOODS

Whole Foods has built a rather radical employee engagement and management system. It empowers its front-line employees to make all decisions pertaining to purchasing, pricing, vendor relationships, hiring, setting salaries, and a whole lot more. Employees are empowered and also held in check by a peer pressure system. Their and their team mates' monthly bonus depends on the performance of their unit. Whole Foods makes all the performance data, within each store and across all stores, available to its employees so they can see how they are doing in comparison to others within the store as well other stores. It has integrated knowledge sharing throughout the organization, so if anyone stumbles across a valuable product or lesson, the information is shared quickly.

ZAPPOS

Zappos is perhaps the best proof of how employee engagement drives innovation. In a little over ten years, Zappos went from zero to over a billion dollars in value. Tony Hsieh attributes Zappos' success to company culture and a committed workforce. A big part of Zappos' operation is its call center, but unlike many other call centers, it has no call scripts. There are no call quotas and there are no escalation procedures. Employees are empowered to use their judgment to help the customer and provide a "wow" service. Zappos hires employees for their passion for service, trains them for four weeks, and at the end of training, offers them $2,000 to quit if they feel they are not the right fit. No questions asked. Zappos challenged everyone to come up with at least one improvement, every week, to make Zappos better. Zappos encourages employees to develop personally and professionally, be humble, be passionate, and have fun.

ZARA

Zara, an innovative fashion apparel retailer out of Spain, has gone unnoticed for over thirty years. However, it has propelled its parent company from a balance sheet near zero to almost $20 billion in net worth in a very cut-throat retail business. The secret sauce behind Zara's success is a new business model that produced trendy clothes in three to four weeks, compared to the traditional nine- to twelve-month development cycles. To stay ahead of emerging trends and respond to local market needs, Zara empowered its front-line employees to spot trends, seek input from customers, and send instant feedback to its in-house designers through handheld devices. This quick feedback to designers keeps them informed about rapidly changing trends and ensures that Zara store shelves are stocked with the trendiest clothing lines. While most retailers rely on their operational efficiencies and tight supply-chain network to compete on cost, Zara built a quick turnaround business model by tightly integrating its on the ground intelligence with the back office.

Appendix B

Recommended Readings

Blue Ocean Strategy: How to Create Uncontested Market Space and Make Competition Irrelevant

by W. Chan Kim and Renee Mauborgne

This book is an excellent source of ideas, inspirations, and strategies for creating new products that make the competition irrelevant through value innovation. In a traditional model, rival companies compete for the same market share in a very head-to-head battle, using strategies like product features, lowered cost, and brand value proposition. These tactics, referred to as "the red ocean," often result in a very bloody battle and downward death spiral. Instead, the authors recommend "the blue ocean" strategy, which makes the competition irrelevant by expanding the market scope beyond traditionally recognized boundaries.

Blue Ocean Strategy provides a six-step framework for value creation and market needs analysis. The book cites examples of companies like Cirque du Soleil, Starbucks, eBay, Yellow Tail, Apple, Southwest Airlines, and Dell Computers, and how they broke the traditional industry mold and created blue oceans of new wealth. The book outlines a simple "create—eliminate—raise—reduce" framework that can be very helpful when contemplating value creation ideas and designing new products.

Disciplined Dreaming:
A Proven System to Drive Breakthrough Creativity
by Josh Linkner

This well-written book provides actionable items that can help individuals, entrepreneurs, teams, and organizations develop creativity skills. The author relates the creativity used in producing jazz music to the creativity needed in running a business. The author conducted over two hundred interviews to develop a five-step framework for boosting creativity at work. The book offers many tools and strategies to tackle different types of creativity challenges.

This book is full of exercises that you can use in your organization for all sorts of business problems. The book outlines the process framework for mind mapping, brainstorming, re-engineering, strategic planning, edge storming, and a number of other techniques used for developing creative solutions to business problems. These techniques can be used in any business setting, and people involved in product development or creative problem solving will find these tools invaluable. The book is also full of ideas for creating a work environment that inspires creativity, collaboration, and out of the box thinking.

Drive: The Surprising Truth About What Motivates Us

by Daniel H. Pink

Drive is a brilliantly written book that brings together a lot of research and case studies to stress the point that the typical carrot and stick management style is no longer effective in today's business environment. This technique worked well in the industrial age where most of the jobs were highly procedural and algorithmic. Today, however, employees face new challenges every day and are called upon to use creativity and pool vast amounts of resources to serve customers and devise novel solutions. These employees are not motivated by money, but rather an innate drive to satisfy their values.

This is a leadership and management book that can help leaders better understand human motivations and how to create an environment where employees are self-motivated. The book offers three principles of motivation—Autonomy, Mastery, and Purpose, and offers tips and techniques to put these principles into action. This book was perhaps one of the earliest management books that set me on my personal quest for employee engagement.

Empowered: Unleash Your Employees, Energize Your Customers, and Transform Your Business

by Josh Bernoff and Ted Schadler

Empowered is an eye-opening book written by two Forrester analysts who pulled together a lot of research and case studies to demonstrate the increasing influence of social technology and how a company can leverage these technologies to serve, engage, and attract customers. Customer service is no longer an isolated department, but rather everyone's job. The book provides a good balance of in-depth analysis, high-level principles, and a framework to unleash employees, energize customers, and transform the business to win over today's empowered consumers.

All companies have a mixed bag of employees—a small portion of them highly engaged, a handful of rogue employees, and a vast majority of them somewhere in between. The book shares a framework for empowering highly engaged employees and creating an environment that pulls the ones in the middle to be more engaged. The book is very inspirational and shares real-life stories of employees who saved the company brand by actively engaging with customers through social technologies, as well as disasters due to a lack of employee engagement and empowerment.

Good to Great:
Why Some Companies Make the Leap...and Others Don't
by Jim Collins

Good to Great is a modern classic of management theory. Jim Collins, together with a team of twenty-one researchers, searched through the performance results of 1,435 companies, looking for those who made substantial improvement and sustained it over time. The researchers finally settled on eleven companies and discovered a set of common traits that made them successful. Jim Collins concluded that it is not a high-profile CEO, innovative business model, the latest technology, or even a fine-tuned business strategy that makes companies great, but rather a corporate culture that promotes finding the right people for the job. Collins concluded that with the right people in the right positions, many of the problems that plague companies and sap valuable resources will automatically dissipate.

Collins attributes long-term success to level five leadership, corporate agility in adopting new business models, a single unified focus toward one core competency, use of technology to extend business capabilities, and a culture that promotes an entrepreneurial spirit and deep-rooted personal investment in both personal work and the company's success.

The Innovator's DNA:
Mastering the Five Skills of Disruptive Innovators
by Jeff Dyer, Hal Gregersen, and Clayton M. Christensen

The Innovator's DNA is a result of an eight-year study conducted by two professors, Jeff Dyer of Brigham Young and Hal Gregersen of INSEAD, under the guidance of innovation titan Professor Clayton M. Christensen of Harvard. The study posed a fundamental question: Where do disruptive innovations come from and what are the traits of people behind the companies that produce disruptive innovation?

Even though the title *Innovator's DNA* suggests innovation skills as an innate capability, the authors make the case that innovators are not born, but made. Anyone can be innovative if he or she practices certain skills. The authors studied some of the most respected leaders, including Steve Jobs, Jeff Bezos, Richard Branson, Mark Benioff, and Google founders Larry Page and Sergey Brin, and concluded that there are five basic traits that enable people to produce disruptive innovations—associating, questioning, observing, networking, and experimenting. The book includes a self-assessment test to discover your own Innovator's DNA and offers practical tips for developing each of the five skills. The first half of the book is focused on developing individual skills and the second half offers helpful techniques to build organization skills. I highly recommend reading this book to sharpen your personal innovation skills and develop your company's innovation discovery capabilities.

The Innovator's Solution:
Creating and Sustaining Successful Growth

by Clayton M. Christensen and Michael E. Raynor

The Innovator's Solution is a sequel to Clayton Christensen and Michael Raynor's best-selling book *The Innovator's Dilemma*, where they introduced the concept of Disruptive versus Sustained innovations. This book is a great read for business leaders, who are more focused on driving top-down strategic innovations. The book offers suggestions on how to make the organization innovation ready by aligning resources, processes, and values, and specific go-to market and execution strategies for both disruptive and sustained innovations.

The Innovator's Solution introduces the concept that customers hire products to do specific jobs and companies should segment markets according to those jobs, and not by product or consumer attributes like geography, demographics, price, etc. The authors make the point that established incumbents almost always emerge victorious in sustaining innovations, but almost always lose the battle in disruptive innovations. Disruptive innovations typically promise a lower profit margin and, therefore, have a hard time succeeding against an established brand that is enjoying high profit margins. The most important lesson for me, as it applies to bottom-up innovation, was to "be patient for growth, but be impatient for profit."

Little Bets:
How Breakthrough Ideas Emerge from Small Discoveries
by Peter Sims

This is one of my favorite books. It demonstrates the power of small changes in a world that is obsessed with the next billion-dollar idea. Peter Sims explains that what appears as one big idea is often a collection of little ideas, and most big breakthrough innovations can be traced back to small, incremental improvements that come together under a common vision. PIXAR, now a multi-billion dollar conglomerate, transformed the movie animation industry, but look closely and you will find its roots and evolution are a direct result of little bets.

Little Bets connects the dots between creative geniuses from various disciplines and argues that all creative types take small, affordable risks to test the market. Experimenting is a way of life for these individuals, and they constantly try new things, observe, learn, adjust, and repeat until they get it right. Great ideas come with tinkering and time.

Selling the Invisible: A Field Guide to Modern Marketing
by Harry Beckwith

Very few high quality books have been written about selling services, even though the service industry accounts for more than

79 percent of United States GDP and over 60 percent worldwide. Even though this book's goal is to teach readers how to market and sell a service, I found it equally resourceful and relevant to service innovation.

The service industry has no physical products that remind customers about the quality or value the company brings. You constantly have to remind customers through every act, every contact, every piece of communication and brochure about your quality and service standards. The book is full of nuggets from basic service quality to market research, planning, marketing, value proposition, pricing, and delivery of the service. This book is a must read for anyone in the service industry or who has a service role.

The Future of Management

by Gary Hamel

If you feel really brave and ready to rock the boat, then pick up this book. Gary Hamel is one of the most respected management professors and thought leaders in the business community. Professor Hamel argues that the management practices prevalent in today's business world are outdated for an information economy. He claims that long-term success does not come from operational excellence, technology, or new business models, but rather management innovation. The book is full of examples of innovative companies like Google, W.L. Gore, Whole Foods, GE, Toyota, and many other leading companies that made radical departures from typical management practices to build very successful companies. This is a very provocative book and will challenge many of your management beliefs and practices.

Notes

INTRODUCTION

- *The New Yorker*, May 16, 2011, *Creation Myth* http://www.newyorker.com/reporting/2011/05/16/110516fa_fact_gladwell

- *The Wall Street Journal*, May 23, 2012, *You Call That Innovation?*, http://online.wsj.com/article/SB10001424052702304791704577418250902309914.html

- Gallup, *State of the American Workplace*, http://www.gallup.com/strategicconsulting/163007/state-american-workplace.aspx

- Gallup, *State of the Global Workplace 2011*, http://www.gallup.com/strategicconsulting/145535/State-Global-Workplace-2011.aspx

- *Switch: How to Change When Change is Hard* by Dan and Chip Heath

CHAPTER ONE

- *The Future of Management* by Gary Hamel
- *Gallup Business Journal,* http://businessjournal.gallup.com/content/163130/employee-engagement-drives-growth.aspx
- *Empowered: Unleash Your Employees, Energize Your Customers, and Transform Your Business* by Josh Bernoff and Ted Schadler

CHAPTER TWO

- *MacNews, Apple pays Creative $100 million in iPod-related lawsuit,* http://www.macnews.com/content/apple-pays-creative-100-million-ipod-related-lawsuit
- *Steve Jobs* by Walter Isaacson
- *The Innovator's Dilemma: The Revolutionary Book That Will Change the Way You Do Business* by Clayton Christensen
- *The Google Story* by David A. Vise, Mark Malseed, and Adam Grupper

CHAPTER THREE

- *The Innovator's DNA: Mastering the Five Skills of Disruptive Innovators* by Jeff Dyer, Hal Gregersen and Clayton M. Christensen
- *The Innovator's Solution: Creating and Sustaining Successful Growth* by Clayton Christensen
- *Wikinomics: How Mass Collaboration Changes Everything* by Don Tapscott and Anthony D. Williams

CHAPTER FOUR

- *Innovation Leaders: How Senior Executives Stimulate, Steer and Sustain Innovation* by Jean-Philippe Deschamps

- *The Google Story* by David A. Vise, Mark Malseed, and Adam Grupper

- *Delivering Happiness: A Path to Profits, Passion, and Purpose* by Tony Hsieh

CHAPTER FIVE

- *Blue Ocean Strategy: How to Create Uncontested Market Space and Make Competition Irrelevant* by W. Chan Kim and Renee Mauborgne

- *Forbes, How Ritz-Carlton Stays At The Top* http://www.forbes.com/2009/10/30/simon-cooper-ritz-leadership-ceonetwork-hotels.html

- *The Idea Hunter: How to Find the Best Ideas and Make Them Happen* by Andy Boynton, Bill Fischer, and William Bole

CHAPTER SIX

- *Switch: How to Change When Change is Hard* by Chip Heath and Dan Heath

- *The Field of Organizational Behavior* by McShane and Von Glinow http://highered.mcgraw-hill.com/sites/dl/free/0078112648/944508/Sample_Chapter.pdf

CHAPTER SEVEN

- *SRI: The massive top secret lab in the heart of Silicon Valley*, http://www.zdnet.com/blog/foremski/sri-the-massive-top-secret-lab-in-the-heart-of-silicon-valley/1837
- http://www.sri.com/engage/innovation-programs
- *Innovation: The Five Disciplines for Creating What Customers Want* by Curtis R. Carlson and William W. Wilmot

CHAPTER EIGHT

- *The Future of Management* by Gary Hamel

CHAPTER NINE

- *The Google Story* by David A. Vise, Mark Malseed, and Adam Grupper

CHAPTER TEN

- *Drive: The Surprising Truth About What Motivates Us* by Daniel Pink
- *Close to the Vest*, http://www.forbes.com/global/2007/0702/028.html
- *A Theory of Human Motivation* by Abraham H. Maslow

CHAPTER TWELVE

- *Good to Great: Why Some Companies Make the Leap...and Others Don't* by Jim Collins
- *Outliers: The Story of Success* by Malcolm Gladwell
- *Mindset: The New Psychology of Success* by Carol Dweck

- *Starbucks Newsroom*
  http://news.starbucks.com/article_display.
  cfm?article_id=225

CHAPTER THIRTEEN

- *The Happiness Hypothesis: Finding Modern Truth in Ancient Wisdom* by Jonathan Haidt
- *The Future of Management* by Gary Hamel
- *The Invisible Gorilla: How Our Intuitions Deceive Us* by Christopher Chabris and Daniel Simons
- *Switch: How to Change When Change is Hard* by Chip Heath and Dan Heath

CHAPTER FIFTEEN

- *The Innovator's DNA: Mastering the Five Skills of Disruptive Innovators* by Jeff Dyer, Hal Gregersen, and Clayton M. Christensen
- *Disciplined Dreaming: A Proven System to Drive Breakthrough Creativity* by Josh Linkner
- *Entrepreneur,* "Pierre Omidyar"
  http://www.entrepreneur.com/article/197554
- http://faculty.eng.fau.edu/shankar/files/2013/02/
  HenryFordAndInnovation.pdf
- *The Idea Hunter: How to Find the Best Ideas and Make Them Happen* by Andy Boynton, Bill Fischer, and William Bole
- *Where Good Ideas Come From: The Natural History of Innovation* by Steven Johnson

Acknowledgments

I have been writing code for computers for much of my life, but this is the first time I've written something this big for humans to read. It would be an understatement to say that it was hard, and I couldn't have done it without the help and support I received from some very special people.

This book would not have been possible without the help of some key individuals and a variety of influencers, and I would like thank them sincerely for all of their help. First and foremost, I want to thank my wife, Simona, for her patience, encouragement, and for putting up with me during the times when I was checked out and lost in my thoughts trying to write this book. She is also my sounding board, editor, and inspiration.

Second, I would like to thank Patrick Snow, my publishing coach and mentor. I couldn't have completed this book without his help.

I also want to thank my editor, Tyler Tichelaar, for making this book readable to humans and transforming my poor writing into a piece of art.

I want to thank Ric Rosario, Ron Parisi, and Jay Stewart for supporting me and encouraging my experiment on the company level.

I also want to give a special thanks to Daniel Pink. His book *Drive* was very instrumental when I was searching for answers to employee engagement issues. He is my mentor, and he has guided me throughout the process of writing this book.

I also would like to thank many of the great thinkers and writers whose books inspired me and taught me everything I have shared in this book, including David Allen, Harry Beckwith, Clayton Christensen, Jim Collins, Carol Dweck, Atul Gawande, Malcolm Gladwell, Marshall Goldsmith, Mark Goulston, Chip Heath, Dan Heath, Chan Kim, Jonah Lehrer, and Brian Tracy.

I would like to thank many friends and mentors who shaped my life and encouraged me in my personal journey of leadership and personal development.

I hope you have enjoyed reading this book and have found it helpful. My goal was to provide you step-by-step guidance on how to create the Bright Idea Box program at your organization so it engages employees and grows the business at the same time.

I invite you to give me your feedback and to ask any questions that you may have about creating this program.

Please feel free to reach me at Jag@IdeaEmployee.com

About The Author

Jag Randhawa is a Technology Executive, Professional Speaker, and Executive Coach. Jag has more than twenty years of technology industry experience with a strong track record of building high performance teams and award-winning products. Jag is a frequent speaker on the topics of Innovation, Employee Engagement, and Leadership.

Jag is the mastermind behind the MASTER innovation program and the founder of Idea Employee Labs, a management consulting company. Jag shares a deep passion for humanity and a desire to make a difference in the world.

Born and raised on a farm in rural India, Jag developed a sense of appreciation for doing the best with what you have, which translated well into the corporate world. Jag started programming in his early teen years and got a full-time job as an engineer at age seventeen after completing his diploma in Electronics and Communications Engineering. Subsequently, Jag obtained a Bachelor of Science in

Information Technology, but his thirst for continuous learning extends from neuroscience to Zen philosophies.

Jag lives in the San Francisco Bay area with his wife, a neuroscientist, and two daughters, whose smiles can melt anyone's heart.

BOOK THE AUTHOR FOR YOUR NEXT EVENT

Jag is available for select speaking, consulting, and coaching.

To book Jag for speaking at your next conference
OR
bring the MASTER Innovation Program into your organization

Contact:
Idea Employee Labs
274 Redwood Shores Parkway, #417
Redwood City, CA 94065
(888) 804-6919
Jag@IdeaEmployee.com

www.TheBrightIdeaBox.com

www.JagRandhawa.com

Index